THE
DUAL BRAIN,
RELIGION,
AND THE
UNCONSCIOUS

THE

DUAL BRAIN, RELIGION, AND THE UNCONSCIOUS

SIM C. LIDDON, M.D.

PROMETHEUS BOOKS • BUFFALO, NEW YORK

Dedicated to both my parents, whom I miss very much.

To Dad, who taught me to reason, to question, and to be open to new possibilities.

To Mother, who taught me to trust and respect both feelings and tradition.

Published 1989 by Prometheus Books
700 East Amherst Street, Buffalo, New York 14215

Copyright © 1989 by Sim C. Liddon

Library of Congress Cataloging-in-Publication Data

Liddon, Sim C.
   The dual brain, religion, and the unconscious / by Sim C. Liddon.
      p.   cm.
   Bibliography: p.
   Includes index.
   ISBN 0-87975-523-7
   1. Psychology, Religious. 2. Split brain. 3. Unconscious.
I. Title.
BL53.L46   1989
200'.1'9—dc19   89-3765
                                                              CIP

Acknowledgments

This book could not have been written without the support, patience, wisdom, and scholarship of my good friend Dr. Gene Fred Taylor. Many a lunch was spent discussing, debating, and generally exploring ideas, including many of those presented in this book. It has been both exhilarating and instructive, and I want to thank him for the experience.

Second, I want to express my thanks and appreciation to my old mentor, Dr. George Engel, who years ago helped shape my intellectual development and with whom I recently shared a creative exchange of ideas.

Contents

8   Contents

Introduction

Psychology, the science of mind, is incomplete as it now stands, for it does not deal successfully with those very attributes that make people most human—emotions, desires, intentions, values, and the like. Neurophysiology has either ignored such areas or deprived them of their humanity by considering them as mere epiphenomena of chemical or physiological processes. Behavioral psychology has excluded them from its interests as not amenable to study. Humanistic psychology has certainly included these areas within its interests, but it has lacked the consistency and discipline necessary for the structured development of a science. And while no such criticism can be lodged against Freudian psychology, its theoretical formulations have neither been accepted by nor integrated into the "hard" sciences.

Perhaps this may be excused, for psychology is a young science; however, there comes a time in the evolution and growth of any science when it has exhausted the conceptual possibilities of its basic ideas and is ripe for a new orientation. Certainly the possibilities of neurophysiology and the behavioral, humanistic, and Freudian psychologies have not yet been exhausted, but they have come far enough for us to see that psychology's present scientific approaches are inadequate. They

9

omit the richness of experience and exclude the passionate aspects of humanity from their domain, except for that lifeless, colorless recognition found in the sterile shell of reason. Experience per se is excluded from scientific understanding.

The apparent justification for this state of affairs is that such phenomena as love, hate, desire, and fear are "just" transient, ephemeral phenomena that by definition are not rational in nature, and as such they must be examined as physiological derivatives if they are to be studied at all. If clergy and theologians want to speak of them as "spiritual" matters and include them in their domain of the "soul," then so much the better. To keep science objective, we must exclude all matters that do not present themselves to our awareness in a rational form.

But can we not look rationally even at those aspects of ourselves that are nonrational and yet not treat them either as mystical phenomena or as epiphenomena? Can we not include nonrational aspects within a rational, scientific understanding that is consistent with physical experimentation and yet treat the rational and nonrational with equal respect? Can we not bring the experiential dimensions of human beings— emotions, desires, intentions, values—into a rational matrix to which the hard sciences need not object, yet not as derivatives of chemical processes?

This book makes an initial attempt to introduce a viable new conceptual framework for dealing with the problem outlined above. That is, the split-brain experiments conducted in the last few decades have given us new information about the human mind, and I attempt to use this data in combination with what we know of the symbolic process. I then examine some possible implications this hybrid of ideas might have for a rational understanding of subjective experience. More specifically, I examine some possible implications this hybrid of ideas has for a psychological understanding of magical beliefs as well as various aspects of religious experience, areas that psychology has for the most part shied away from in the past.

The crucial question to be addressed by psychology has to do with how it might appropriately extend itself into areas that are purely subjective and experiential in nature without being transformed into mere metaphysical speculation. After all, the cannons of science demand that its theoretical constructs be objectively tested against objective fact, but how can psychology call itself a science if the subject matter is as ephemeral as beliefs, values, and decisions?

In addition to the conventional approaches already employed, psychology can establish through experimental research (i.e., research with split-brain subjects) the basic mode or modes used by the human mind to organize subjective experience and then use this insight to understand human experience in areas less amenable to experiment (e.g., religious experience). However, would this not simply be argument by analogy? I think not, for all that falls within the human conscious awareness—from being aware of a visual image during a psychological experiment to experiencing "the sacred"—fall within the same conceptual category, that of psychological (mental) experience. The mind's basic modes of organization are common factors to human subjective experience, whether it be called religious or psychological or what-have-you; and this gives science a conceptual bridge for the study of both magical beliefs and religious experience.

PSYCHOLOGY AND RELIGION

In an effort to provide a rational analysis of those subjective and experiential aspects of the human being that do not present themselves in rational form, I have focused on magical beliefs and religious experience. But in doing so, I am venturing into forbidden territory because science has for the most part been content to leave the passionate side of humankind to others, most notably to artists and theologians. Conversely, organized religion has been, one might say, the chief benefactor (or perhaps victim) of science's forfeiture of interest in feeling experience. (The term *feeling* is used throughout this book to indicate those "felt" experiences which are not sensory in nature—e.g., our emotions, desires, values, passions, intentions, and so on.) The religious community has attempted to create its own matrix of rational understanding that would make feelings consistent with its own supernatural assumptions. The approach of this book is decidedly different, for I will use reason in an attempt to make supernatural beliefs consistent with psychological observations of the human being. In doing so, I hope to encourage psychology to be less timid in expanding into areas traditionally left to others, for only then will it be complete.

A problem arises whenever one tries to speak of religion in any generic way, for the field is so broad that, as James said, "It would indeed be foolish to set up an arbitrary definition of religion's essence, and then to proceed to defend that definition against all comers" (1903, p. 35). However, James went on to say that this need not prevent one from choosing a particular aspect or meaning from all the many possible meanings and focusing one's attention on that area. In the tradition of James, then, I acknowledge that what

I have to say about religion speaks only to certain aspects (albeit crucial aspects) of what is included in the broad range of meanings associated with the term *religion*. For those who find my particular meaning too narrow, I can only ask their indulgence.

This book may well challenge the religious assumptions of some, but it is not, as might appear at first glance, anti-religious or anti-God. In fact, it may afford those skeptics among us who cannot accept the traditional formulations of organized religion a way of reconciling their need for an expression of religious passion with their need for reasoned observations of the world. Such an approach may eventually allow them to be included within religion's pale, if they can fashion for themselves a religious belief that is consonant with their own skeptical nature. If ever a theology is fashioned that is acceptable to an empiricist, it may well begin with ideas similar to those presented here.

THE GESTALT APPROACH

Science approaches its fields of study in two very different ways: the first starts from single observations and builds relationships between them into a larger, more complex structure; the second grasps the wholeness to begin with and then deciphers and identifies the individual constituent parts. The latter is the approach of the Gestalt psychologist, for instance, who feels that when grasping the whole, one has something more than merely the sum of the parts. The integration itself adds something extra: a new form or Gestalt that was not apparent before the formation of the larger view.

The approach of this book can be understood as consistent

with the latter view, for I have attempted to integrate the works of a number of scholars into a consistent whole with the belief that only such an integration can expose a pattern that would otherwise be lost. I feel that the integration of these individual ideas into one unified whole, into one Gestalt as it were, adds a new and exciting dimension, which would be lacking if each idea were to be taken separately. Truth does not come only in small packages.

A central theme of my discussion is in a very basic sense an extension of a suggestion made years ago by James, namely, that a "science of religions" be established. It was his thesis that a personal religious experience represents an "invasion" from the unconscious. And because the concept of the unconscious was fairly well established and might be accepted by the other sciences, James felt it might serve as a basis for a new science having connections with the other sciences. His suggestion, however, fell on deaf ears. The behaviorists objected to the concept of the unconscious, and the neurophysiologists ignored it. In the intervening decades, the idea has faded even in the minds of the more psychodynamically minded psychiatrists and psychologists. True, efforts have been made on a sociological level to establish a science of religions; but in the sense that James intended, there has been no successful attempt to establish a science of religion grounded on the concept of the unconscious.

Perhaps the main stumbling block to such an effort has been the fact that "the unconscious" needed to be more precisely defined and understood. It needed to be conceived in some fundamental way and grounded on an even more basic idea. Freud's and Jung's attempts to do this have not been acceptable to science generally, and it has seemed that James's lead ostensibly led nowhere. In the pages that follow, I have, for all practical purposes, tried to take the batan from the point at which James left it over eighty years ago, and one of the first orders of business is to reexamine the concept of the unconscious and to define it more precisely—to ground it within a broader context. Beginning with data from the split-brain experiments, which suggest that the human mind organizes data in two fundamentally different modes, I proceed to view this idea in the light of our insights about the symbolic process. These ideas are interwoven until we arrive at a theory of the unconscious.

The overall intent is to look for a *natural* as opposed to a *supernatural* interpretation of magical beliefs and other religious phenomena. That is, it is an initial effort to fashion an understanding of at least some (not all) aspects of religious experience, which is *natural* in the sense that it is based on observations of human beings themselves as opposed to *supernatural* in the sense that it assumes supernatural entities and powers. And in the process we find a happy surprise, for we arrive at an understanding of the unconscious that seems very pertinent to a seemingly unrelated field, i.e., psychotherapy. We find, for instance, during the therapeutic hour clinical evidence of these two modes of mental processing symbolically expressing the individual's subjective experience in dreams and neurotic symptoms. Certainly this is not new, for Freud noted all this years ago, but what is exciting is that it can now be seen as part of a larger context that includes both experimental research and observations from a variety of other fields. This, then, reflects a remarkable concordance between psychotherapeutic (and psychoanalytic) material and neurological experimentation that must arouse the curiosity of even the most skeptical positivist. Let us assume that the legitimacy of ideas is enhanced when they fortuitously corroborate other ideas in seemingly unrelated fields. Then the ideas presented here concerning symbolism, mental processing, and the unconscious are substantiated as they apply to magical beliefs and religious experience because they are consonant with the clinical observations and insights of dynamically oriented pychotherapists. They are substantiated because they bring seemingly unrelated areas within the same structure of understanding. There thus exists the possibility that aspects of psychotherapy, psychiatry, neurology, anthropology, religion, and philosophy may be seen as lying within the same context of understanding.

WORDS OF CAUTION

In order to keep our perspective clear, several precautions should be taken. The first is to not over romanticize the notion of left-brain/right-brain differences, since this dichotomy has become a runaway and undisciplined effort to explain all sorts of phenomena and cultural differences.

The second is not to throw the baby out with the bathwater: the split-brain experiments have shown differences, and it would be unfortunate if we chose not to explore the implications of these differences just because of the potential for abuse by those who would misuse the information. There may be a tendency to pass up the opportunity to look at the organization of subjective experience per se until all the anatomical questions have been answered, but this would be a mistake.

The third point of caution—one that may help in understanding the differences that have emerged with the split-brain experiments—is that one must make a sharp distinction between psychological experience and anatomy. I give much attention to the fact that the mind seems to process information in two different ways, via a linear (or analytic) mode and a gestalt (or holistic) mode. However, a problem and a controversy arise if one attempts to correlate these differences with anatomical features of the brain. Whereas some may correlate the linear/gestalt differences to the left and the right cerebral hemispheres respectively, others suggest that this left/right correlation is more apparent than real (Gazzaniga 1985). Moreover, the initial interest in left/right differences has now been replaced by attention to how the two hemispheres interact—whether they are inhibitive, facilitative, complementary, or independent, for instance. Furthermore, there is now more interest in *intra*hemispheric distinctions, such as differences between the anterior and posterior or medial and laterial aspects of the brain, dysfunctions within the hemispheres, as well as possible dysfunctions in the subcortical/cortical relationships (Kinsbourne 1988).

No matter how these anatomical questions are settled, the linear/gestalt differences in the organization of subjective experience still seem to hold. An analysis of function is needed on a number of different levels: psychological, anatomical, biochemical, and physiological levels, to name a few. The linear/gestalt distinctions in the human organization of experience is an analysis of psychological matters, and we should not be discouraged from making the most of such distinctions even if there remain unanswered questions, or if dichotomization has occurred too freely on other levels.

The point is, the best way to appreciate the psychological data that has emerged from the split-brain experiments is through the linear/gestalt perspective, even though the anatomical questions may eventually be answered in one of several ways. Certainly, one would want eventually to correlate psychological matters with anatomical, biochemical, and physiological matters, but things will have to evolve considerably before this is possible. At this point one must make a clear distinction between the various levels of analysis so that the anatomical, biochemical, and physiological controversies do not cloud our understanding of psychological matters.

A fourth point of caution is to not discount the apparent linear/gestalt differences in subjective experience by assuming such a formulation is too reductionistic. If indeed there is such a dichotomy in how the mind organizes experience, then one would indeed find evidence of its existence in a wide variety of phenomena. The fact that the evidence is widespread only supports the contention that the linear/gestalt differentiation is indeed extremely basic.

Lastly, we should remember that what is presented here is only one way of approaching the mind's organization of subjective experience; and while it seems rather exciting (to this author at least) in its implications, there may now be and in the future there surely will be other legitimate approaches. Such is the way of the human mind's endless capacity to extrapolate; but this should not keep us from appreciating and exploring the possibilities of this particular approach.

THE BOUNDARIES OF THIS DISCUSSION

If what follows can be viewed as a Gestalt, then it can also be conceived as analagous to one's field of vision where details are clearly seen only within a very small focal point that rests within a much larger peripheral and less clear context.

If so, then, the focus is on a psychological understanding of magical beliefs and religious experience as functions of bimodal mental processing, the symbolic process, and the unconscious. At the same time, however, a larger, less clearly defined context is implied, which includes various aspects of psychology, psychiatry, psychotherapy, science, neurology, philosophy, and related fields. This larger context remains less clear as attention is focused on a few concepts and principles.

The major aspects of the split-brain experiments are several decades old, and the experts in the field are now as concerned with anterior/posterior, medial/lateral, and sub-cortical/cortical differences and dysfunctions as they are with left/right hemispheric distinctions. The text by James is over eighty-five years old and that by Otto over seventy. Both Cassirer's and Langer's remarks are certainly old hat to the professional philosopher, and it might well be questioned why I have relied so heavily on such dated material when there are so many new thoughts concerning science and the human condition, i.e., Polanyi (1958), Heilbroner (1980), Ravetz (1971), Popper (Levinson 1982) and Kuhn (1970).

First of all, I feel that some of the conceptual possibilities of the older works are only now emerging as we consider the psychological implications generated by the split-brain research. And second, as stated above, I have had to narrow and restrict the focus of what I am trying to say. I am not trying to review what has been generally said about science and humanity. I suggest some ideas that should be significant for a rational and scientific look at certain selected aspects of religion, yet I do not try to present a summary of the science of religion. I have not, for instance, even referred to the mammoth amount of work contributed by The Society for the Scientific Study of Religion, and I have not used the contributions by numerous scholars interested in psychology (and psychiatry) and religion. Likewise, reference to authors within humanistic psychology, an area intimately akin to the subject matter presented in this volume, will be almost entirely lacking, as will references to other related areas such as computerized models of symbolic thought and those psychological studies dealing with curiosity and exploratory behavior. Even more glaring will be the lack of attention to the issue of faith as given by theologians. And I only briefly mention the voluminous work in contemporary psychoanalytic thought dealing with object relations as well as the extraordinary work by Jung and his cohorts dealing with symbols as they relate to religious and psychological issues.

Much of my work is based on the ideas of Gestalt psychology, yet I will give only slight attention to the experimental work in perception done by Gestalt psychologists, and none at all to efforts at relating Gestalt psychology to the psychotherapeutic situation. Nor will I attend to the large amount of work done with Gestalt therapy per se. I speak of the magical thinking of primitives, yet I leave completely unexplored the magical thoughts of children as well as the works of Piaget and discussions of the developmental aspects of human thought. Likewise, I have spent much time and effort discussing language and how it relates to an individual's world view and to his sense of reality, yet I do not refer to the important contributions of the linguists, such as the transformational model of Chomsky (1958). I speak of language and psychotherapy, yet I do not refer to work relating language to psychotherapy (Bandler & Grinder 1975). I speak of conscious awareness, the unconscious, one's sense of reality of the world, psychosomatic disorders, split-brain research, etc., yet I do not refer to the penetrating thoughts of such scholars as Sperry (1976) and Pribram (1976) as they relate both to conscious awareness and to the mind-body quandry.

All of the above are important areas, but in this particular work I want to focus on a more specialized (and manageable) area, namely, the integration of the psychological implications of split-brain research with the concept of the symbolic process. In considering a few implications this might have for magical beliefs and religious experience, I am making only an initial reconnaissance into the area of subjective experience. There are numerous implications for other excursions as well, as witnessed by the length of the list above, but their exploration will have to wait.

Part One

Voodoo
and
Split-Brain Research

1

Voodoo Death, Believing, and the Modern Need for a Unity of Thought

VOODOO DEATH

I have seen more than one hardened old Haussa soldier dying steadily and by inches because he believed himself to be bewitched; no nourishment or medicines that were given to him had the slightest effect either to check the mischief or to improve his condition in any way, and nothing was able to divert him from a fate which he considered inevitable. In the same way, and under similar conditions, I have seen Krumen and others die in spite of every effort that was made to save them, simply because they had made up their minds, not (as we thought at the time) to die, but that being in the clutch of malignant demons they were bound to die. (Cannon 1942, p. 169)

"Voodoo Death," with all its images of evil spirits and black magic, was the title of a paper published in 1942 by

Cannon, whom many considered one of the most creative and careful physiologists of the twentieth century. After studying accounts from all over the world, such as the quotation above by Leonard, Cannon committed himself to the reality of this strange and seemingly mysterious mode of death.

People today tend to consider such accounts as apocryphal and to write them off as lacking in "hard, scientific data." This is all the more tempting in the light of the fact that primitive societies of the sort reported on in the past may no longer exist. However, Cannon was certainly not naive with regard to "hard data," and the fact that, after careful study, such a sophisticated scientist was convinced of the reality of Voodoo death is a compelling inducement to take the phenomenon seriously.

A related point argues in the same direction: numerous accounts in the anthropological literature compose a mosaic of evidence supporting the idea that various primitive peoples all over the world developed world views, creation stories, and accounts of the world's existence that are in some ways extraordinarily consistent with one another. The fact that this mode of experiencing the world, called "mythical thinking" in the anthropological literature, is described so consistently suggests that such conceptions of the world reflect humankind's capacity to view the world in a way decidedly different from that of our modern, Western experience.

This difference seems to have important implications for a psychology of humans and must therefore be examined closely. The thesis suggested here and to be argued in later chapters is that the human constitution is disposed toward two basically different ways of utilizing the symbolic process. Furthermore, depending on which of these two modes of processing predominates, one arrives at two entirely different

world views characterized by different and incompatible notions of time, cause, and identity. The effects of the predominance of one or the other of these two modes of mental
processing are present in our modern world, although their
influence is not so easily appreciated. Indeed, the world views
represented by these two modes assume historical importance
in that they underlie the age-old discussions concerning two
ways of "knowing," and they also reflect the differences between "the sacred" and "the profane." The differences between
the conceptual worlds of religion and science, and the latter's
more recent progeny—psychology—can be understood as the
result of these world views. In other words, some of the
determinants of the age-old conflict between science and
religion as well as the present day differences between psychology and religion are present in each of us today in the
form of a conflict between tendencies toward two different
and incompatible modes of "believing."

I shall now examine some of the reports of "mythical
thinking" and how they contrast with the logic of our everyday
world. A second report cited by Cannon concerned the
Aborigines of northern Australia. When an individual was
known to be the victim of black magic and was therefore
known to be condemned to die, all his relatives and friends
withdrew their support and treated him as if he were already
dead. They would ignore him, exerting a social pressure upon
the victim to take the only escape left, death. The individual
would cooperate and make no effort to participate in group
activities, eventually withdrawing into a "death" illness. The
community would perform rituals and ceremonies accorded
to the dead, and the victim, in a highly suggestible state,
would respond to the group's suggestion and die.

There are numerous examples in the literature of the

extraordinary power of believing among primitive people. One such story, reported by a South African and collected by Levy-Bruhl (1928, pp. 44–48), concerned two natives, S and K, who went into the woods to gather honey. S found four big trees of honey, but K could find only one. The latter went home complaining of his bad luck, while S returned to the woods to bring back his honey. Alone in the woods, however, he was attacked by a lion and torn to pieces. S's relatives went to the witchdoctor to find out who was responsible for his death and were told that K, out of jealousy, had turned into a lion and had killed S. The accused denied this, and the tribal chief declared that the matter should be decided by ritual. The ritual proved unfavorable and K, confronted with the overwhelming case against him, confessed and was tortured.

It seems apparent that K could not have taken the form of a lion, and it appears that he became the victim of his tribe's miscarriage of justice. This was not the opinion of anyone at the time. The accusation, while a bit far-fetched to the civilized mind, was natural to all concerned: S's family, the witchdoctor, the chief, the crowd of natives gathered around, and even K. Their framework of understanding did not include the concept of accidental death, and since S had been killed there had to be some "cause" for it, such as the jealousy of K. The latter at first denied the charge but, confronted with the fact that he was the logical suspect and that the oracle had found him guilty, and knowing that his tribe had also found him guilty, K was unable to resist the overwhelming evidence and confessed. The whole system was reinforced in the minds of the villagers, and the way was prepared for the next occasion when one of them might fall within the jurisdiction of tribal justice.

How could these things have happened? How could someone be convinced against his own senses that he had turned into a lion and had devoured his friend? How could someone die from voodoo? Our first impulse, on reading such accounts of voodoo death, sorcery, and witchcraft, is to be fascinated, so foreign are these experiences. The second impulse is to forget them, and with a knowing smile write them off as characteristic of "uncivilized and primitive" thought processes, having little or nothing to do with our own cultured, logical, and precisely perceptive "civilized" minds. "But," Levi-Strauss (1966) might say, "the primitive is just as careful and precise in his thinking as we are, only he thinks along different parameters." And Levy-Bruhl (1975) might add that we are really not so far removed in our own thinking and that the kind of thinking we see in primitives can be found in civilized humans as well.

If we take seriously what Cannon, Levi-Strauss, Levy-Bruhl, and numerous other anthropologists and linguists say, then we must look carefully at these "primitive" belief systems. Certainly any psychological event powerful enough to result in death within a few hours warrants attention. Cannon himself speculated that voodoo death might be caused by overactivity of the sympathetic nervous system; fifteen years later, Richter (1976), from observations of wild and domesticated rats, argued that voodoo death was more likely caused by a parasympathetic overactivity. However, neither Cannon or Richter looked carefully at the more psychological aspects of the experience, i.e., the believer's world view and the activity of "believing" as a powerful influence even in today's "civilized" world.

BELIEVING: MORE THAN A "RATIONAL" EXPERIENCE

What is "believing," if it is as powerful as just described? This is not a simple question; the best minds have been at a loss to explain it. Hume, in the appendix of his *Treatise of Human Nature* (1739), confessed his great difficulty in being able to describe or precisely define the concept of *belief*. He resorted to saying that it consisted of a certain "feeling," which he called a superior "faculty" or "solidarity" or "firmness," but he acknowledged that he could not find just the right words to express its meaning (Hume 1888, pp. 628–629). The many philosophers who followed have not done much better.

The point of this discussion is to justify the idea that the act of "believing" is not merely a rational experience but also an affective or "feeling" one. In spite of the fact that we see evidence daily of people who hold irrational beliefs, the layman in Western societies is inclined to think of "beliefs" as a set of rationally defined statements. Certainly our "professional thinkers," our philosophers, have not been so inclined, for those within the philosophy of science have shown that scientific "reason" is as laden with subjective experience as nonscientific "reason" (Polanyi 1958, Kuhn 1970), but most of us must adjust a bit to conceive of "believing" as something so amorphous as feeling.

Since James (1903) first looked at what he called the "faith state," there has been precious little interest in "believing" among psychologists. (Possible exceptions to this would be those clinicians and investigators interested in hypnosis and in the placebo effect.) The Freudians have had other interests, and of course the "faith state" could not be explored by the behaviorists, since the concept did not fall within their defined area of interest, behavior.

It is precisely this state of affairs that poses a problem today. To follow the behaviorists as representatives of science, we miss an important part of the human experience of "believing"—feelings. To follow the lead of the neurophysiologists, we find that feelings are merely epiphenomena and secondary to chemical processes, and "believing" per se is a concept that lies outside of a physiological frame of reference. On the other hand, theology, and especially Christian theology, has had much to say about the feeling aspects of "believing" in its formulations about "faith." But its assumptions about absolute truth, divine revelation, and the like do not allow for a careful and logical analysis of the experience. It is as if we must choose between a point of view that does not really recognize feelings as causative factors in human behavior and one that does but whose rational formulations are encumbered with assumptions about supernatural forces and entities. If, as I will suggest, we are to look at religion in a psychological way and if we are to bring all of experiencing into one unified whole, what is needed is an approach whereby we can reason about and carefully analyze such concepts as *feeling, deciding, valuing,* and *believing* and yet remain free of organized religion's hidden assumptions.

In order to navigate our way out of this confusing situation, I will argue for a "unity of thought" whereby all of experiencing can be brought within one context of understanding. The reader may well wonder how I could first suggest two basically different modes of experiencing and then argue for a "unity of thought." This indeed is an important point, and my response is that it is only because these two modes of mental processing and experiencing the world are so distinct that there *can* be a unity of thought. Only by recognizing that there are other products of mental processing besides reason, can we reason about areas that have heretofore been relegated to "mystery" and other unfathomable dimensions. Only by recognizing that there are other ways to use the symbolic process besides the linear, discursive mode of logic and language, can we use logic and language to understand those other forms, such as art, religious rituals, and myths (Cassirer 1955). Certainly there are aspects of experience that lie outside of reason's grasp, but let us reach as far as we can before capitulating to "mystery" as an explanation.

THE MODERN NEED FOR A UNITY OF THOUGHT

In ancient Egypt, the scarab compacted balls of dung and rolled them along the ground; in these balls it laid its eggs. The Egyptians believed that the larvae that later emerged came forth miraculously self-created. They considered the scarab to be sacred, seeing it as a mystical symbol of the sun god, for they believed that the great sky beetle, Khepra, like the little dung beetle, appeared self-created each day to roll the ball of the sun across the sky (Smith 1952).

The early Pueblo Indians knew that their religious rituals kept the father, the sun, in his daily path from the east to the west. They knew that if their ceremonies were interrupted it would destroy all creation, since the father in the sky depended on their rituals for his continued journey. Thus the Pueblo Indians, knowing that the survival of the entire world depended upon their actions, had a meaning for life for which no modern humans could ever hope to have (Waters 1963).

Medieval humans knew that the heavenly bodies were

kept in their orbits by angels, and religious scholars of the time knew that because God created humans in his own image it was only natural that the earth, where humans resided, was supremely important and at the center of the cosmos. Medieval science was based on medieval religion, and there was no conflict in the views of God, man, and nature (Russell 1974).

Modern Western humans, if they think of it at all, view the universe in natural rather than supernatural terms, seeing the Earth as a small planet revolving around an insignificant sun lying at the periphery of a galaxy in a universe containing millions of galaxies. Modern science has introduced a new framework of understanding, and average modern Western humans (if there are such creatures) simply do not believe, cannot believe, in the same way as average eighteenth-century American Indians or average medieval European humans. For the latter two groups, every aspect of life centered around their religious beliefs. Individuals knew from whence they came, why they were placed on earth, how to conduct their private and business lives, and what they might hope for in the afterlife. Their passions and their science were all within the same framework of understanding. For modern Westerners, this is simply no longer the case, and it is the absence of this guiding value base of religious influence in modern life that led both Nietzsche and Bonhoeffer—atheist and Christian, respectively—to speak of the "death of God." For modern Western peoples, who live for the most part in a profane world, religion has lost its meaning. It is not so much that in their everyday transactions they consider religious beliefs to be wrong; it is simply that (in spite of lip service to the contrary) they do not consider them at all.

For better or for worse, we are greatly influenced by a

"profane" world view that is extraordinarily successful in analyzing and predicting natural events. At the same time, however, something has been lost to us, a passionate sense of our connection with the infinite and a sense of our own importance in the cosmos. We have lost a structure of meaning and significance that allows us to identify who we are and where we stand in the order of things. We have lost the sense of worth that comes from knowing that we and our deeds are part of an ultimate good.

In spite of what one might wish to the contrary, we cannot return to the former state of understanding. We can only acknowledge that something is missing within this profane existence of ours. We can accept that with the loss of our ability to vividly "experience the supernatural," we have also had to forfeit the meaning and sense of worth that it afforded. It seems that with this forfeiture we experience vague, free-floating anxieties and nagging doubts about the meaning and direction of our lives, our values, and our priorities.

In the two thousand years since Aristotle first championed the laws of logic for discursive reason, we have almost come to the point of considering rationality to be the very essence of the human mind, especially in the last several hundred years with the spectacular success of science and its method. One point I emphasize is that rational thinking is indeed unique to humans, but only as a derivative of a more generic unique-ness, the human ability to symbolize (Cassirer 1955). Because we have either ignored or looked with condescension upon the products of symbolizing other than reason, we have ignored whole dimensions of experience. We have failed to understand the importance of *feelings* in believing, in valuing, and in constructing our world view. What I have just said was more eloquently expressed by the philosopher Cassirer, but the significance of what he said has never been fully developed by psychology. Indeed, it is a tragedy that Cassirer's ideas were never reconciled with those of his two contemporaries, Freud and Jung, the two greatest figures within psychology to be interested in the symbolic process. Perhaps the present discussion will be a step in that direction.

THE LINEAR MODE OF PROCESSING

Over the years, Western culture has become almost exclusively rational in its outlook, seeing the world through the eyes of a reasoned, sequential mode of symbolizing as best exemplified by language and mathematics. Here facts are presented like beads on a string, one after the other, and their significance or meaning depends upon a particular syntax or order of presentation (Langer 1980). I call this mode of processing or handling information, which I shall explore further in chapter 2, the linear mode of mental processing. I will point out in later chapters that it has a major influence on our ability to analyze and to discriminate and compare intellectually, and it exerts its influence by being the primary influence in one of humankind's great cultural efforts to understand both itself and the world—science (Cassirer 1955). In fact, its influence has become so paramount in Western culture that it has almost excluded from legitimacy any component of "believing" or meaning other than reason and logic per se. But what happens if experiences do not lend themselves to an analytical approach? For instance, when we listen to Mozart, no amount of analysis will ever lead us from the length of the sound waves to the joy of the listening. Similarly, when we view a beautiful sunset, no amount of analysis will lead from the wave length of the electromagnetic radiation to the thrill of experiencing the splendid sight. To rely exclusively on the analytic approach of reason, we cut ourselves off from the possibility of integrating all of our experiencing into a unified whole.

The significant point at this juncture is that modern, Western peoples have a need for a unified system of experiencing and thinking that integrates all of subjective experience, both reason and feelings, into one consistent whole. (I shall explore this in more detail in chapter 8.) Individuals need, but do not have, a context of understanding that includes a theory both of human nature and nature generally that allows equal and legitimate stature to reason per se, on the one hand, and to the symbolic expression of intentions, emotions, values, and the like on the other.

THE GESTALT MODE OF MENTAL PROCESSING

I shall show in chapter 2 that evidence converging from a variety of separate and independent sources bears on this issue of a gestalt mode of mental processing. It supports the idea that in addition to the linear mode of mental processing, as exemplified by the linear or sequential presentation of language and mathematics, there exists a "holistic" or "gestalt" mode of mental processing. Here one synthesizes and brings constituent elements together from all directions, as it were, into a form such as a visual image (a cross, or a skull and crossbones). In this case, appreciation of significance and meaning come from instantaneously grasping the form as a whole and in its entirety, instead of sequentially, like the words in a sentence. Evidence for such a "holistic" or "gestalt" mode of mental processing has been independently suggested by (a) neurologists in their study of brain-injured patients, (b) behavioral psychologists, (c) philosophers as they rationally analyze human mental productions, (d) anthropologists studying the beliefs of primitive peoples, (e) neurosurgeons and experimental psychologists studying the mentations of neurosurgical patients, and (f) psychoanalysts in their study of dreams and neurotic symptoms. This, indeed, is extraordinary: that a similar idea has been concluded independently by such a variety of apparently unrelated (and at times antagonistic) disciplines, and it certainly adds credence to their mutual conclusion.

A significant point, to be more fully developed later, is that our perceptual images are used to symbolize our feelings, and thus the gestalt mode of processing that is involved in the creation of sensory images is very much involved in the symbolic expression of feelings. Both feeling and reason find expression, one in a form that is more gestalt and the other in a fashion that is more linear, but because of our present-day emphasis on the products of reason we do not fully appreciate the legitimacy of feelings and the importance of the gestalt mode of processing.

BIMODAL MENTAL PROCESSING

Of specific import here is that, with this convergence of ideas, we have the opportunity to explore the implications for the development of a unifed system of believing. If we conceive of reason itself as being an example of the linear mode of mental processing, and if we use the term *bimodal mental processing* to include both this linear mode of processing and the gestalt mode of processing, then this concept allows us a fresh and expanded view of "believing" that would include not only reason and logic but also feelings and values as symbolized through the gestalt mode of processing. Moreover, bimodal mental processing combined with ideas about the symbolic process, I shall maintain, produces a pivotal hybrid of ideas that serves as a nodal point for including aspects of psychology, neurology, and religious phenomena within the same framework of understanding. It is hoped that scientific thought and religious experience will eventually become integrated for us, as for the Pueblo Indians and for medieval humans, and all of experiencing can be brought into a single whole.

"A unity of thought" implies a matrix of reasoned and logical understanding, yet humans are as passionate and feeling as they are rational. Thus, "a unity of thought," while it must of necessity be discursive and rational, must not reduce all "legitimate" experience to reason per se. It must allow legitimacy to those other areas of human existence that cannot be expressed in the linear, sequential form of reason. It must allow for the expression of values, desires, intentions, and emotions and yet understand them as something other than mysterious, mystical matters. It must steer between the temptation to reduce all legitimate expression of human experience to reasoned formulations, as some extremists in the scientific, positivistic community might be prone to do, and the temptation to resort to miracles and mystery to explain those experiences that cannot be expressed in logical terms, as some in the religious community may tend to do.

Because our Western culture overemphasizes the analytical, linear mode of mental processing, one of the difficulties we have is that of understanding and appreciating the products of the gestalt mode of mental processing, something hard to identify in our culture. To help with this, I have attempted in this chapter (and will again in chapter 4) to examine the thinking of primitive peoples, for there we shall find a world view and belief system where the influence of feelings and the gestalt mode of mental processing predominate. It is hoped that by looking at what is more obvious in others we might better view that which is not so clearly seen within ourselves. Furthermore, we shall find that the beliefs of primitives, which are so very different from our own in many respects, resemble in those very same respects the mode of believing characteristic of religious experience.

All this might be relegated to the "interesting but inconsequential" category were it not for the fact that it provides a background for the principle discussion and thesis to follow. It is an effort to give that thesis significance within a context that is larger and closer to home than might first appear. Modern, Western humans need to integrate their reason and their passions, their science and their sense of worth, into one unified matrix of understanding. The individual needs to find a sense of meaning in life and a sense of value in actions. This book is an attempt to proceed in that direction.

2

Split-Brain Experiments
and the Duality of Human Nature

Every age has its own preoccupation, and every age of great
intellectual achievement has its own new "generative idea,"
according to the philosopher Langer (1980). She suggests that
we have now exhausted all such past ideas. The time is ripe,
she maintains, for the next great idea to initiate a new
generation of creative thought, and she further suggests that
we have just such an idea in the concept of "symbolism."

Not only have the engineers and experimental scientists
relied on symbols, for the concept has been the very basis
of mathematics, but also logicians and psychologists have
used them. Whether symbolism will in fact be the next "generative idea" is yet to be seen, for since the proposal was
first made by Ms. Langer in 1942 there seems to have been
less than a spectacular "generation" of ideas. Psychology and
psychiatry have turned to other horizons, such as behavior-
ism, community psychiatry, biochemical and other somatic

therapies, "rational" and "experiential" therapies, and formulations about "object relations" and "the psychology of the self." In fact, it would seem that within psychology and psychiatry there has been a general decline of interest over the last several decades in the conceptual possibilities of "symbolism." I will examine it from a different perspective.

While over the last several decades interest in the symbolic process has been declining, at the same time an exciting new field of research has developed. Psychologists, working with both animal and human subjects in whose brains the neural connections between the hemispheres have been severed, have made a number of intriguing observations. I am suggesting here that we can integrate this "split-brain" research with what we know of the symbolic process and, in so doing, gain a great deal from this hybrid of ideas. We will find that just as there are two modes of processing information corresponding generally (but certainly not specifically) to the left and the right hemispheres, so there are two ways of experiencing a symbol, corresponding generally (but not specifically) to the scientific approach on the one hand and the approach of art and religion on the other. Furthermore, these two ways of experiencing a symbol lead to the two different world views represented generally (but not specifically) by the logical and scientifically consistent world of the modern, civilized cultures on the one hand and the magical, supernatural world of the primitive on the other.

As presented, the statements above are too dichotomizing; they relate to general correlations, which I make for heuristic reasons. In actuality things are not that clear-cut. The anatomical distinctions are not so clear that each mode of processing is restricted exclusively to either hemisphere, for the evidence is that both modes function in each of the two hemispheres and they ordinarily function together in any case. And science is not so clearly free of "feelings" and subjective experience as some would like to think (Polyani 1958, Kuhn 1970). Nor are primitive cultures lacking in logical thought forms (Levi-Strauss 1966), but it does seem apparently true that the world view and thinking processes of the primitives seems to allow for emotions and feelings to enter into their view of reality to a relatively greater degree than is true of someone guided by the scientific approach of our modern cultures.

But to get back to the point I was making, I suggest that the integration of the work from the split-brain research with the concept of symbolism affords us a new perspective that was previously lacking. In fact, I suggest a variation of Langer's remark about symbolism's being a new generative idea. That is, I suggest that the concept of "bimodal mental processing" combined with the concept of symbolism may be a "generative hybrid of ideas," especially for psychology, psychiatry, and religion.

THE SPLIT-BRAIN EXPERIMENTS

The human brain, like the brains of higher animals generally, is double, having two hemispheres connected by a band of neurons called the corpus callosum. What would happen if the connections between the two hemispheres were cut? Would humans, in fact, have two minds? As amazing as this sounded several decades ago when it was first proposed, we now have evidence suggestive not only of two minds but perhaps a multiplicity of minds (Gardner 1983, Gazzaniga 1985). Perhaps it remains to establish just how many "minds" one has, but there is indeed good evidence that the human mind is not a single, homogeneous unit.

Experiments with cats have demonstrated that when the corpus callosum is cut, each hemisphere functions independently and as if it were a brain within itself. The separated hemispheres have been trained independently so that each selects a different response to the same situation (Myers 1965, Sperry 1961, 1967, Myers & Sperry 1953). That is, each hemisphere solved the same problem in a different way. Subsequently, it was demonstrated that monkeys, surgically altered in a similar way, could solve independent problems simultaneously and in a way far superior to that of monkeys having had no such operation (Trevarthen 1962, Gazzaniga & Young 1967).

The demonstration that severing the corpus callosum in animals seemed not to impair their functioning encouraged neurosurgeons to cut the connective band in human subjects who had been diagnosed with uncontrollable epilepsy in the hope that an epileptic discharge in one hemisphere could be prevented from spreading to the other. The operation proved to be successful, with the control of the epilepsy augmented, and to all outward appearances there was no change in the patients' personalities, intelligence, or general make-up. (Actually, the first such operation was performed some years earlier by Van Wagenen, but its use was resurrected after the animal experiments, at which time the patients were studied more carefully for psychological sequelae.)

To be more accurate and precise as to the consequences of this neurosurgery, these subjects were asked to participate in some rather creative experiments by psychologists under laboratory conditions. And on closer examination, there were indeed subtle alterations in these individuals' mental functions (Sperry 1964; Gazzaniga, Bogan & Sperry 1965; Gazzaniga 1973). Subjects reported seeing lights when they were flashed in such a way as to be received by the left hemisphere, but not on the opposite side. It might be suspected that the right hemisphere was in effect blind, but that proved not to be the case. The right hemisphere controls the left hand but not the right, and visa versa; and when the subjects were asked to point to the lights with the respective hand instead of reporting verbally, they could respond quite accurately. This suggested that the subjects' previous failures to give verbal responses were due to the fact that the motor control of speech was located in the left hemisphere. But the right hemisphere could do more than identify the presence of lights, as demonstrated by other subjects. A picture of a spoon was flashed to the left hemisphere and it was identified verbally, but when it was flashed to the right hemisphere one subject denied she had seen anything at all. She was then instructed to reach under the screen with her left hand and select by touch alone the object she had seen on the screen. After palpating each of several objects hidden from view, she correctly chose the spoon. Her left hemisphere "knew" the object verbally, yet the right hemisphere "knew" it by touch but not verbally, a rather curious fact suggesting that under some circumstances one can express what one knows via a mode that is not available under other circumstances.

This speculation makes several other experiments all the more intriguing. In one experiment a subject was shown two pictures: a chicken's claw was flashed to the left hemisphere and a snow scene to the right hemisphere. From a group of pictures the subject was asked to indicate with the respective hand which picture he had just seen. He selected with his left hemisphere the picture of a chicken to go with the picture of a chicken's claw, and with the right hemisphere he selected the picture of a snow shovel to go with the snow scene. However, when asked why he had made these particular selections he responded, "That's easy. The chicken claw goes with the chicken and you need a shovel to clean out the chicken's shed" (Gazzaniga & LeDoux 1978, p. 148). In this case it seems that the left hemisphere used its superior language faculty to compose a "logical" or plausible reason for the selection made by the right hemisphere. From working extensively with such patients, Gazzaniga speculated that the right hemisphere is capable of expressing its own feelings and preferences through its own "separate mental system," i.e., separate from the mental system of the left hemisphere. The latter tends to elaborate its own verbal "reasons" that are at times spurious and at odds with that of the right hemisphere. This certainly makes one wonder just how much of what we believe to be our basis for doing something is primarily a rationalization of choices and positions assumed for other than "logical" reasons.

THE RIGHT HEMISPHERE AND VISUAL-SPATIAL TASKS, ART, AND EMOTION

While the left hemisphere seems to have obvious superiority with respect to language, the right hemisphere seems to be superior with respect to visual-spatial tasks. Bogan, one of the neurosurgeons who performed the split-brain surgery, had patients copy simple designs, like a cross or a cube. These patients, in spite of the fact that they were right handed, could copy designs much better with their left hands, suggesting that the ability to recognize and integrate forms into a

"whole" was a specialized function of the right hemisphere.*
One of the more dramatic demonstrations of this was in a
film by Gazzaniga and Sperry. The subject was presented
with cubes having two red sides, two white sides, and two
sides divided along the diagonal half red and half white. The
subject was to arrange these blocks so as to form patterns
identical to designs shown on a series of cards. The film first
showed the subject arranging the blocks successfully with the
left hand, but when he tried to do it with the right hand
he had a great deal of difficulty. He struggled, seemingly
conflicted with indecision and confusion, and at one point
the left hand entered the picture and tried to help the right
by turning the cube to the correct position. The investigator
firmly removed it and the right hand went on fumbling with
its task (Springer & Deutsch 1981, p. 44).

The superiority of the right hemisphere seems not to be
limited to visual-spatial tasks. From the study of patients with
unilateral brain damage. Head (1963) suggested, "We know
very little of the behavior of auditory images in (the loss
of the ability to express oneself with language due to left
hemisphere injury) but the direct reproduction of melody and
the recognition of time and tune are not affected." Later studies
supported this observation, showing the right hemisphere to
be far superior to the left in tonal and timbre and melody
recognition as opposed to notational recognition, which seems
to be a left hemisphere function (Milner 1962, Chase 1966,
Shankiweiler 1966, Kimura 1964). And strange as it may seem,

---

*Throughout this discussion it will be assumed that a person's dominant hemisphere
is the left hemisphere and the dominant hand is the right hand. This is done for the sake
of simplicity of exposition, when, of course, it is not true for everyone. In some people,
for instance, the language centers are in the right hemisphere and the left hemisphere is
better suited for visual-spatial tasks.

some patients with damage to the left hemisphere have suffered the loss of speech but can sing songs from memory or even, in one case, conduct an orchestra (Benton & Joynt 1960, Henschen 1926, Critchley 1966).

Alajouanine (1948) reported the case of a famous musician, Maurice Ravel, who at the height of his career suffered a stroke. His "analytic recognition" of musical notation (a function of the left hemisphere) was impaired along with his language ability, and this grossly hindered his piano playing and musical sightreading. However, his melodic, rhythmic, and stylistic sense was unimpaired, allowing him to play or sing by memory. It was suggested that he had even accentuated the intensity and sharpness of his artistic realizations suggesting to Alajouanine that the aphasic and the artist lived together on two distinctly different levels. However, the simple left/right distinctions are not so clearly differentiated, for other reports suggest that the situation is more complicated. While some evidence (Head 1963) seems to confirm the left/right distinctions, others do not (Wertheim & Botez 1961, Marin 1982, Luria et al. 1965).

Likewise, it would be wrong to say that the right hemisphere has no capacity for language. Indeed, Restak (1984) suggested, "The right hemisphere seems to contribute the color, the verve, the 'firepower' to ordinary speech. In addition to puns and wordplay, it makes possible the expression of enthusiasm, joy, sadness, and despair" (pp. 259–260). He went on to refer to neurological patients with damage to the right hemisphere who had difficulty comprehending the emotional content of verbal expressions, which suggests that the right hemisphere's superiority in artistic endeavors entailing musical and form recognition is accompanied by an ability to recognize emotional content. This special relationship between the right hemisphere and emotional experience is supported by the work of several other authors (Dimond & Farrington 1977). In one study, emotionally charged films were found to be more disturbing when projected, via special lens, to the right hemisphere of normal subjects. Another study compared subjects' brain activity as detected by an electroencephalograph while they read two types of reading material, technical material and folk tales (Restak 1984). The results indicated that reading either of the two materials activated the left hemisphere, as one might expect, but the folk stories, more rich in imagery and emotional connotations, activated the right hemisphere as well.

TWO MODES OF PROCESSING INFORMATION

The experiments with split-brain subjects do have drawbacks: they are few in number, they deal with subjects who already have pathological processes going on (i.e., epilepsy), and the operation interrupts the normal functioning of the intact brain. However, the results of these experiments are supported not only by animal experiments and studies of patients with unilateral brain lesions, but also by experiments with normal subjects using a variety of other techniques. While more study surely needs to be done, some judgments have been made by those working in the field. First there is the obvious thought that the two hemispheres are specialized for different cognitive functions. Second, it has been concluded that the primary factor in hemisphere specialization is not the type of information considered (i.e., words or shapes or sounds) but how the brain processes information.

In trying to interpret this data, however, there is controversy. The anatomical distinctions between the left and right hemispheres are not as clear-cut as they appeared during the first few years of the split-brain research. Indeed, it seems that the way the lay public and popular press "explain" an infinite variety of lifestyles in terms of left/right differences is "simple minded" and a distortion of good scientific research. Let us assume that there are anatomical distinctions that must yet be clarified and that the left/right distinction does represent an oversimplification. With this in mind, and for heuristic reasons, let us go on to look at the differences and distinctions as they appeared during the first years of this research. No matter how the anatomical questions are eventually answered, there are distinctions in human mental (or psychological) functioning that are both legitimate and important. In what follows I will speak of left/right differences because that is the easiest way to present the psychological material, but the reader should recognize that the anatomical distinctions are not so clear-cut. The point is, it is vital to distinguish between psychological matters and anatomical matters, and we are primarily interested in the former. Keeping this in mind, let us go on to review some of the results from the split-brain research.

It appears that the left hemisphere processes information in a way that is superior for relating and comparing separate items and for processing information in a *linear* or sequential mode. It is a far superior mode for language; for the appreciation of time, number, and logic; for the expression of analytic thought; and for the precise discrimination of details and differences. In short, it serves the analytic and scientific "purposes" of humankind. This I shall call the *linear mode* because it allows us to examine relationships in a linear way. For instance, the equation A + B = C is essentially a way of understanding in a linear form the relationships between the symbols A, B, and C. Its two outstanding characteristics are, first, the appreciation of separateness and discreteness of individual items or facts and, second, the recognition of linear relationships between these distinct items.

Continuing with the "simple-minded" approach of left/ right differences, it seems that the right hemisphere synthesizes rather than analyzes. It appears to process information by instantaneously bringing together or integrating different parts into a unified form, or "whole," and is superior in dealing with simultaneous relationships and global properties. It is suited for producing our sensory images of the world as well as the images of our imagination and dream life, and is more suitable for the symbolic expression of the emotional component of our subjective experience. I call the mode of processing associated with the right hemisphere in this "simple-minded" approach the "gestalt" mode, which has two outstanding characteristics. First, there is an instantaneous or simultaneous bringing together of different data or facts into a unified whole, best exemplified by the figures of the Gestalt psychologists. They demonstrated that one perceives a form as a whole and that at the same time there is a lack of awareness of the parts when one focuses on the whole form. The second characteristic is the lack of ability to compare or differentiate, which naturally follows from the fact that when one's attention is focused on the whole gestalt, there is a lack of awareness of the parts. While the left hemisphere serves humankind's scientific needs, the right is superior for artistic and religious expression.

For heuristic reasons I have been talking in anatomical terms about "left" and "right" brain, but let me reiterate that *the anatomical distinctions are not so clear as I have sug-*

gested. For my purposes, the focus is on identifying the *functional* aspect of these two modes of mental processing, not their exact anatomical correlations. In other words, each hemisphere shows at least some evidence of both modes of processing, but the split-brain experiments have made it possible to identify the two *functionally* different modes of processing information. *Thus the important distinction is not so much between the left and the right hemispheres as it is a functional distinction between the two modes of mental processing.* I shall collectively refer to these two *functionally* different modes as "bimodal mental processing."

THE DUALITY OF HUMAN NATURE

The idea of a duality within human nature has been expressed in art, literature, and philosophy for many years. Now it has been grounded in the experimental approach of modern science. There seems to have been a progression from the initial experience of intuitive insights to a reasoned analysis of those insights, and then on to a position where intuition and reason are supported by experimental research. This represents a model of the creative integration of these two modes of mental processing that has characterized progress in Western knowledge generally. After their collaborative efforts to know the world generally in this way, perhaps these two modes of processing are now ready to know themselves.

A whole host of creative and careful thinkers have, as Bogan (1973) suggested, espoused the idea that "man is possessed of two ways of thought (which present themselves in) the form of . . . a struggle between reason and emotion" (p. 120). Moreover, the two different modes of organizing experiential data have been independently described with such extraordinary consistency by individuals of diverse backgrounds that it gives credence to the legitimacy of the basic phenomenon they all described. Thus we have these two modes of organizing experience described by anthropologists like Levi-Straus (1966) and Levy-Bruhl (1975); by philosophers like James (1890), Langer (1980), Cassirer (1955), and Northrop (1979); by Polayni (1958), a chemist working in the area of the philosophy of science; by psychoanalysts like Freud (1961) and Fenichel (1945); by behaviorists like Pavlov, Sechenov, and Luria (Bogan 1973, p. 122); and by neurologists like Head (1963).

Let us look a little closer at how some of these scholars describe the two basic modes of mental processing, one of a verbal or linear nature and the other of a "pictorial" or "gestalt" nature. For instance, Northrop, in *The Meeting of East and West,* a very scholarly book published in 1946 (well before the time of the split-brain experiments), clearly identified the two modes of mental expression described here. His terminology was different but the scope of his scholarship was very broad, and he correlated these two modes of thought with the thinking characteristic of the oriental and occidental cultures. From reviewing the work done on split-brain patients, Ornstein (1972) reached a similar conclusion. He suggested that the technical, rational thought of the West overemphasizes those functions associated with the left hemisphere, whereas the cultures of the East, with their intuitive and mystical insights, emphasize those functions related to the right hemisphere. We are here less interested in anatomical differences between the left and right hemispheres than we are in the psychological or functional distinctions between the two modes of mentally processing data. Keeping this in mind, the work of Ornstein reinforces the scholarship of Northrop, who was totally and completely un-concerned with brain anatomy in any case.

Langer (1980), a philosopher, perhaps looked as carefully as anyone at these two modes of organizing data; a brief look at her work will show just how similar her thoughts are to the ideas subsequently reached by the scientists who experimented with split-brain subjects. She suggested that two different kinds of symbols mediate meaning in two different ways. What she called "discursive" symbols are exemplified by words, which, when presented as sentences, can express meanings that can be successively understood. However, only experience that lends itself to this type of sequential presenta-tion can be understood by discursive symbols. The second kind of symbol, which Langer called "presentational," presents itself to our awareness as a sensory image, taking the form that our perception takes. Its elements are presented to our awareness in a totality and through a simultaneous presenta-tion, rather than successively like the words in a sentence, and its meaning is understood only with the perception of the form in its entirety. Langer went on to indicate that discursive symbols lend themselves to the analytic approach of science, while presentational symbols convey a rich emo-tional component of meaning, which make them well suited for musical, artistic, and religious expression. (In the next chapter I will formulate some ideas about the symbolic process that are slightly different from those of Langer, but it is impor-tant to mention her ideas here because they were formulated in 1942, before the split-brain researchers eventually formu-lated their own ideas along similar lines.)

Pavlov spoke of "two signaling systems," which, according to Bogan (1973), may well have stemmed in part from a knowledge of Seche-nov's suggestion, quoted and supported by Luria, that the cerebrum has two basic forms of integrative activity: orga-nization into "simultaneous and primarily spatial groups"; and into "temporally organized successive series." (p. 122)

Moving to the other extreme—from those psychologists who had a strong behavioral orientation to the psychoanalysts—we find that Freud also suggested that human thought occurs in two basic modes, "primary process" and "secondary pro-cess," and his ideas generally correlate with those of Luria and Sechenov, the behaviorists. Fenichel (1945), representing the psychoanalytic viewpoint, described primary process as "carried out more through pictorial, concrete images (and) is remote from any . . . logic. But it is thinking nevertheless because it consists of imaginations according to which later actions are performed" (p. 47). Furthermore, he emphasized that the "pictorial language" of primary process thinking, as experienced (for instance) in dreams, is "less fitted for objective judgment," because it is "relatively unorganized, tolerates and condenses contradictions, and is ruled by emotions and hence full of wishful or fearful misconceptions." It is, he maintained, primitive, magical, undifferentiated, archaic, vague, regressive, and primal. Secondary process, he suggested, "is based more on words" (p. 47). When comparing what the behaviorists had to say with what the psychoanalysts theorized, along with the longstanding antagonism between the two groups, it is extraordinary that they should, in fact, agree to such a remarkable degree about these two modes of "thought."

In his curiosity about the duality of the mind, Bogan, the neurosurgeon who was instrumental in much of the split-brain research, collected a "variety of related opinions from various sources" (1973, p. 119) that substantiate the observation that human mentality is in fact bimodal in nature. He pointed out that Ruesch and Kees (1956) suggested that humans think simultaneously in two different modes: one being discursive, verbal, and logical (the digital codification), and the other being nondiscursive, nonverbal, or eidetic (the analogic codification). Bateson and Jackson (1964) used the same terminology. James (1890) spoke of a dichotomy of the mind in terms of "differential" versus "existential." Pribram (1962) also distinguished the "digital" from the "analogic," and suggested that the maintenance of stability in the concept of space utilizes a different mechanism from that providing a stability in time. Goldstein (1960) divided mental functioning into "the abstract attitude" and "the concrete attitude." The neurologist Head (1963) spoke of the "symbolic or systematic" versus the "perceptual or nonverbal" modes. Bogan (1973) himself suggested the "propositional" versus the "appositional," while Humphrey and Zangwell (1951) spoke of the "symbolic," "propositional" versus "visual thinking and imagination"; and Hecaen et al. (1963) spoke of "linguistic" versus "preverbal." These are only a few examples of formulations that have been reached by a variety of precise and careful thinkers describing the same basic phenomenon, giving an overwhelming aura of validity to the idea of bimodal mental processing.

In spite of the massive amount of scholarship supporting the idea underlying bimodal mental processing, it has not, unfortunately, received general acceptance. While scholars and academicians are perhaps aware of its importance, it seems safe to say that the concept has not been of pragmatic importance and has had little effect on how the general public conceives and understands the world. This is perhaps because of our Western preference for reason and the products of a linear type of processing and our prejudice against the intuitive, emotionally laden products of the gestalt mode of mental processing. We might just be predisposed to think of a unity of the self and prejudiced against anything that suggests the contrary. Or perhaps it is because bimodal mental processing has, until the last few years, lacked grounding in experimental science. It is to be hoped that the grounding of this idea in the split-brain experiments will in the future help dissolve our prejudices and help establish the general acceptance of bimodal mental processing. If we think of "believing" as being the product of the joint action of both modes of processing, then we can agree that believing is in fact bimodal, involving both the linear and the gestalt mode of processing. (And everyone but the philosophers "knows" that the same is true for "knowing.") Depending on which mode predominates, one arrives at a world view consistent with that of science or that of religion.

Up to this point I have been speaking of "mental processing" without trying to be more precise. The next step is to clarify what this means, especially as it relates to differentiating these two modes of processing. It seems apparent from the examples already given that there is ample evidence for a dichotomy of mental processing, but the exact nature of the difference between the two modes remains unclear.

In the next chapter, I shall suggest a rationale for understanding this difference, and in doing so I will follow the lead of Cassirer and Langer and focus on perhaps the most crucial and unique element in human mental life, the ability to symbolize. It is this ability that makes the mental life of humans different from that of our animal cousins, and it also appears to be conceptually useful in understanding the relationship between the linear and the gestalt modes of mental processing.

3

Symbolism and Language

Just what is a symbol? On the surface this seems easy to explain. In the expression $A + B = C$, "=" is a symbol signifying that the values on the left side are equal to the value on the right. The image of a skull and crossbones is a symbol for death. The cross is a symbol for Christ, who is in turn a symbol of suffering, redemption, salvation, etc. for Christians the world over. To a Freudian analyst a dream element, such as the loss of teeth, might symbolize castration. The color red is at times a symbol for anger or heat or danger. But how are these meanings connected? How are they related? For most ordinary people with ordinary intellects the shared features in these various applications of the concept "symbol" are not clear. Indeed, like so many other concepts that we take for granted, the meaning of "symbol," which appears so clear at a distance, dims as we approach, and vanishes altogether when we try to articulate it precisely.

If, as Cassirer (1955) suggested, we assume it is true that the essential human action in mental processing is the act of symbolizing, then this is an action that is not accessible to other animals. With this in mind, let us examine how a human being's mentation differs qualitatively from that of our animal cousins, and then go on to examine how this uniqueness relates to bimodal processing.

THE DIFFERENCE BETWEEN
SYMBOLS AND SIGNALS

Pavlov demonstrated years ago that a dog can be conditioned to respond to signals and to repeat actions at the sound of a bell or at the flash of a light. But only humans have the capacity to use signs not only to *indicate* or signal things but also *to represent them.* At the sound of footsteps a dog might perk up his ears and begin to look for his master; the footsteps *signal* the approach of the master. But with humans it is different. As a human hears the approaching footsteps, the individual can *think about* the friend whose footsteps he hears. The word *food* might be used as a *signal* for the dog to expect to be fed, to salivate, and to secret gastric juices. But only humans can *think about* the soon-to-be-had supper, with associations of previous meals, particular foods, etc. Symbols indicate ideas or images of things, while a signal points to the thing itself. Out of the great flux of sensations that flood an individual, humans can fix (or stop or hypostatize) an image and *think about it,* as opposed to merely responding to it. Used in this way, a footstep, or a word for that matter, can function for humans as a symbol as well as a signal.

To examine with more clarity the human ability to symbolize and how our mentation differs from that of our animal cousins, let us look at an experiment by the Gestalt psychologist Kohler (1925). His apes could use a stick to reach a banana outside their cage, so long as both the fruit and the stick could be seen at the same time. However, if the ape had to turn his eyes away from the banana in order to see the stick, he could not use the latter to gather in his lunch (Kohler, 1925, p. 37). It was as if he could not look at the one and think about the other. It seems he could not examine the relationships between the banana and the stick unless they were simultaneously visible.

Imagine, if you will, Kohler's ape muttering (or thinking), "banana, banana," to himself as he turns away from the banana to look at the stick. If such were the case, one can well imagine that the ape might be able to use the stick to pull in the banana. Being able to have the two concepts together—that of the banana and that of the stick—he would be able to compare and examine their relationships. But unfortunately apes do not mutter. It is as if the ape does not have the capacity to store the concepts of "banana" and "stick" within his memory, and thus he is unable to benefit from being able to examine and compare the two.

The crucial factor, then, in human mentality is this ability to stop or "fix" an experience so that it can be examined, compared, and "thought about." If so, just how does this relate to bimodal mental processing? The symbol itself is an image that is associated with this "fixed" experience and allows the latter (in a sense) to be "reexperienced." There are at least five distinct aspects of symbolizing. (1) The process of synthesizing data into a "whole": when this involves sensory data it means synthesizing sensory cues into an image or form, such as a cross, a Star of David, or a skull and crossbones. (2) The synthesizing function is, however, independent of the content of that which is synthesized and can involve experience other than sensory data. That is, emotions and other feelings or a mixture of experiences can be integrated into an *experiential gestalt*. It would seem that this much an ape or a dog can do. (3) Then there is the basic process of "fixing" an experiential Gestalt. (4) There is also the relating of the "fixed" experiences, the experiential Gestalt, and the sensory image. (5) Finally, there is the process of relating or recognizing relationships *between* symbols, as is best exemplified by language and mathematical expressions such as $a + b = c$ or $\frac{a}{b} = \frac{c}{d}$. The gestalt mode seems primarily related to steps (1) and (2), while the linear mode is primarily involved in step (5).

Stated most succinctly, the "gestalt" mode of processing is concerned with organizing data into an "experiential Gestalt" and a sensory image, or symbolic form. These two are then associated so that the image "symbolizes" the experience. The linear mode is involved in relating these "fixed" experiences or ideas in a linear way, making it possible to appreciate their relationships, as with language, logic, and mathematics. The symbol itself is created via the gestalt mode, while the linear mode is concerned with the appreciation of relationships between the created symbols. In the case of an ape, as long as the sensory cue is within the ape's sensory field, it can be related to an experience. But it would also appear that for the ape it is "out of sight, out of mind." (We shall never know for sure, of course, for we shall never have an ape, a crab, or a parmecium tell us so. But this fact alone is enough to convince me that the latter three do not "think" about such matters, i.e., do not use the linear mode to relate symbols.)

WORDS AS SYMBOLS

The phenomenon of "fixing" or "holding on to" an experience is clearly demonstrated in language, for a word "fixes" something in experience and makes it available for memory. More correctly, a human being can "fix" or retain an experience, which is most obvious with words. In this case a word becomes the nucleus of an experience about which whole occasions can be recalled and then related or compared with other experiences.

To explore further the use of words as symbols, let us look at a rather famous passage in the autobiography of Helen Keller (Langer 1980, pp. 62–63). Here she described her first awareness of the power of words, i.e., their power to allow her to conceive or think about specific objects. Keller had previously learned to expect certain things and to identify certain people and places, but on that particular day she *discovered language!* She discovered that a particular act of her fingers constituted a word and that this word "stood for" or denoted something in her physical environment. On that day Keller's teacher took her for a walk, during the event described below occurred.

She brought me my hat, and I knew I was going out into the warm sunshine. This thought, if a wordless sensation may be called a thought, made me hop and skip with pleasure.

We walked down the path to the well-house, attracted by the fragrance of the honeysuckle with which it was covered. Someone was drawing water and my teacher placed my hand under the spout. As the cool stream gushed over my hand she spelled into the other the word water, first slowly then rapidly. I stood still, my whole attention fixed upon the motion of her fingers. Suddenly I felt a mystic consciousness as of something forgotten, a thrill of returning thought; and somehow the mystery of language was revealed to me. I knew then that w-a-t-e-r meant the wonderful cool something that was flowing over my hand. That living word awakened my soul, gave it light, hope, joy, set it free! There were barriers still, it was true, but barriers that in time could be swept away.

I left the well-house eager to learn. Everything had a name, each object which I touched seemed to quiver with life. That was because I saw everything with a strange, new sight as it came to me. (Keller 1936, pp. 23-24)

In this remarkable passage we can see, described in an extraordinary way, the dawning of language in a human mind. We see, through Helen Keller's experience, that words are more than *signals:* they are what help the individual to think about events, allowing him to conceptualize about himself and the world and at the same time appreciate relations, properties, parts, and distinctions.

DENOTATION, CONNOTATION, AND BIMODAL MENTAL PROCESSING OF WORDS

When Helen Keller associated the letters w-a-t-e-r with the substance water we see the denotative function of words. The word *water* denotes the substance water. It is suggested that the linear mode of processing, which allows for discreteness and separation, is involved in the denotative component of our symbolic functioning. Furthermore, that which we shall call the connotative function of a symbol can be seen as a product of our gestalt mode of processing, although its demonstration is a bit more subtle.

From Keller's quotation it is apparent that she had memories from previous walks. Perhaps she was aware of a memory of proprioceptive sensations as she walked through the fields or waved her arms, and certainly she was aware of the sensory experience of feeling the warm sunshine or perhaps the cool breeze or of smelling the honeysuckle. Without debating this point, it seems clear that Keller "knew" or was "aware" of something. Had Keller known the letters w-a-l-k and had she associated that word with the anticipated walk, then the whole of that awareness with all of its associations, including the joy itself, would be included in the *connotations* of the word *walk*. Using a different image, we can imagine that the memory of the discovery of language remained with Keller throughout her life and was associated with that word *water*. That whole experience, the image of the scene, the memory of the touch of her teacher's hands, even the joy and excitement itself undoubtedly remained for Keller part of the *connotations* of w-a-t-e-r. These experiences are gathered into a whole and symbolized by the word itself, certainly representing a more rich and full meaning of the word for Keller than merely its *denotative* meaning of water per se. This "gathering into a whole," even though it involves more than sensory data, is also a function of a gestalt mode of processing.

One point that emerges from the preceding discussion is that an experience (experiencing) can be "fixed" in the mind as a "whole" or as an "experiential gestalt." With a word like *water* we have a clear example of something being "fixed" because its denotative function is apparent, since there is some "thing" or substance denoted. However, for any particular individual all of his own connotations to the word *water* are also retained and associated with the word itself. Not only are "things" fixed but so is the entirety of one's subjective experiencing—e.g., one's emotions, one's sensing of the world, one's thinking, etc.

If the retaining (or fixing) of an experience in the form of an idea or image is what sets human beings apart from other sentient life forms, then the use of words as symbols facilitates that ability. For Helen Keller the word *water* undoubtedly became a symbol of the experience of discovering the magic of language. The word itself became an element about which the totality of the experience could be organized. For this kind of meaning, it is as if a matrix converges upon a particular item, a matrix of connotations (and new connotations to each particular connotation, etc.) that relate the whole of the experience to a particular element. When one's attention is focused upon that element, it can be said then to "symbolize" the whole experience. Furthermore, this gathering together of connotative elements into a central focus—into a symbol—is the product of the gestalt mode of mental processing. The importance of these ideas will become more apparent in chapter 7 where the relationship between conscious awareness and the unconscious is discussed.

Any other item of Keller's experience might also have served as a symbol for the experience, such as the sensation of cool, running water flowing over her hand, or the smell of moisture in the air, or the experiencing the movement of the water pump, or even the joyous feeling and excitement of discovery. Which particular element would more successfully serve as a symbol, as a focus for connotations, might well be determined by factors not well understood, like other connotations to that particular element. And, of course, a particular symbol can symbolize more than one experience, as is the case in both poetry and dreams. The symbol, then, "stands for" or "means" the whole of the experiential gestalt, the whole of the gestalt of connotations that have been brought together via the gestalt mode of mental processing. The idea of an experiential gestalt will be one of the topics addressed in chapter 7. When we focus our awareness on a symbol, be it an object (like a cross) or even behavior (like a religious dance), the connotations symbolized are only vaguely within our awareness and in a way that can be thought of as secondary or subsidiary to that which is within the focus of our awareness.

LANGUAGE AND SYMBOLIZING

If a word is a symbol, then what about a sentence? The latter is in fact more than a group of words, for it has a linear structure that makes it an example par excellence of the linear mode of mental processing. It has grammatical structure, and while this structure is not a symbol in itself, it does tie several symbols together, each with its own particular connotations. Thus a sentence is a complex association of terms whose meaning is a particular constellation of all of the words involved. A sentence tells of a *particular* state of affairs. "Pepper (my family's pet spaniel) licked Nicole (my daughter)" indicates something different from "Nicole licked Pepper." With nouns we have concepts of things, but with a sentence, with words in a linear combination, we conceive of a situation. (A sentence could also be viewed as a "whole"—as a gestalt—for example, when we imagine Nicole and Pepper licking one another. In such a case we "paint pictures with words," and the sentence can be translated, in a sense, into image form.)

Language (especially the family of Western Indo-European

languages) has a form that requires us to order our words or elements, to line them up like beads on a string, one behind the other. This property of verbal symbolism is known as *discursiveness,* and only experiences that can be so arranged can be expressed in a sentence. Any experience that does not lend itself to this form of expression is ineffable, non-communicable via words. Our clearest formulations of exact expressions are discursive in nature and when we speak of the "laws of logic" we are referring to experience that lends itself to this form of presentation.

Symbols functioning via the gestalt and the linear modes of mental processing each allow for a type of meaning that is only poorly expressed by the other. The gestalt mode of processing is the mode we have for symbolizing the feeling content of our subjective experience—fears, hopes, desires, hates, sorrows, loves, passions, guilts, etc.—while symbols experienced via the linear mode of processing allow for logic, discursive expression, and the appreciation of structure and relationships. (We shall see in chapter 7 that this corresponds to the two components of our world view.)

SYMBOLISM AND NON-DISCURSIVE SUBJECTIVE EXPERIENCE

What is the meaning of those phenomena in our subjective experience that lie outside of our discursive understanding, phenomena that include our fears, hates, passions, wishes, loves, desires, guilts, sorrows, and the like? This important question has been approached from two opposing perspectives: that which reduces all meaning to discursive meaning and that which would fill the gaps in our discursive understanding with speculations about magic, mystery, and supernatural entities. Is there some other alternative, one that finds significance in something other than discursive reason per se or ineffable mystery? In the several sections that follow, I will introduce the concepts of "objectification" and "adifferentiation," which will prove useful in constructing an alternative approach to this dilemma.

OBJECTIFICATION

If we were to reduce our concept of meaning and understanding to its linear or discursive form, anything that could not be expressed in this form would also lack the character of symbolic expression. Many of those who stumble over this problem of how to deal conceptually with our subjective experience allude to a vague notion of "intuition" to explain the gaps in our discursive understanding. Others explain the unknown by assuming (conjuring?) supernatural or mystical formulations. They invoke the powers of witchcraft or magic, or they suggest the activities of a god or a "spirit" for that which is not readily translatable into discursive logic. An emotion is symbolized as an image: for instance, fear might be symbolized as the image of a witch; this image is then experienced as "real" and in the "real world." The phenomenon of experiencing symbols of subjective experience as "real" and in the "real world" I shall call *objectification*. (The psychoanalyst might say that because "the differentiation of self-images from object-images" [Kernberg 1980, p. 26] has never been completed, the individual has a tendency to experience his "internalized" objects—his mental images of the world— as objects *in* the world.) This then works conjointly with the mind's searching for a one-to-one cause-and-effect relationship between items in the world (a product of the linear mode of processing), which results in the belief in magical or "supernatural" entities that cause events in the world to happen. In doing so, these persons express their own subjective experience as "objects" or "powers" or entities within the world itself—a most important phenomenon for both psychology and religion. But to do so means letting our sense of reality be determined by our feelings rather than be observation and logic; it means that our own mental images are accepted as ultimate reality.

ADIFFERENTIATION

Another phenomenon, one that is perhaps only a variation of what I have called "objectification," is *the inability to distinguish a symbol from that for which the symbol stands.* This phenomena I shall call *adifferentiation,* a term chosen because it would appear that instead of there being an equating of the two (the symbol and that which is symbolized), it seems more likely that in fact there has never been a separation. When an individual from a primitive culture experiences a particular place as being taboo, as a place of abject fear and terror, there is no distinction between the place and the emotions, between the place as a symbol and the emotions for which the symbol stands. The place is *alive* with feeling. For those Christians who experience the bread and wine of Holy Communion *as* the body and blood of Christ, there is no distinction between the symbol and that for which it stands. Nor is this distinction evident when a worshiper of any religion experiences "the Holy." Reality and the emotion it conveys are one and the same. It might seem more appropriate to say that this experience of "oneness" remains amorphous and undivided and that there has never been a differentiation into an "outside thing" and an "inside feeling." It would seem that this experience is more archaic than discursive reason, which analytically chops experience into an outside and an inside, into "thing" and emotion. The Christian who is capable of experiencing "the Holy" when contemplating the cross and all of its concommitant connotative feelings of redemption, salvation, grace, and the like, finds it hard to "explain" such an experience to a profane mind. In this last example, it would be easy to say that the cross symbolizes thoughts and rational concepts about Christ. It would be easy because, in our thinking, we ordinarily assume that words and concepts are consistent with rational concepts. But notice how dry and uninvolved it sounds to say "The cross symbolizes the thoughts and rational concepts about Christ." How devoid of feeling this is! It might be a descriptive statement of a particular relationship, but it is far from a testament to the drama of the experience itself. It seems legitimate to say that when language reduces something to logical and rational concepts, it reduces or deemphasizes the "feeling" of the experience and robs it of its rich coloration of emotional meaning and significance.

We have at least two modes of mental processing and therefore two ways of experiencing symbols. In the linear or "rational" mode there is discreteness and separation between the different symbols. When the engineer examines his dials or the mathematician reviews his equations, symbols are experienced; and with language, words are symbols that get processed linearly.

In the gestalt mode of mental processing, where a differentiation is present, the symbol and the experience for which the symbol stands have never been separated; the symbol itself "is experienced" in the sense that there is no distinction between it and the experience per se. There is "oneness" or unity of the symbol and the experience: here feeling rather than reason defines "reality." Perhaps it is rather difficult to reason or be logical about this nonrational experience, but to do otherwise is to accept reality as being defined only by our emotions.

I have spoken of two different modes of processing information: one that creates a symbol and another that appreciates linear relationships between symbols. The question arises now as to how all of this presents itself in our everyday life. It should be emphasized that in each of us both modes of processing always function together. It is not hard to see evidence of the linear mode, for any mathematical expression (such as $A + B = C$) offers a clear example. Our concept of cause, as expressed in the sentence "Because of gravity the apple fell to the ground," has a linear form, as does our concept of time, which is seen as demarcated along a linear progression of ordered sequence. Our Western Indo-European language has a linear syntax that demands a particular order to express a particular meaning.

But what is not so easy to see is how our thinking is affected by the gestalt mode of processing. To clarify this point, I shall return (in chapter 4) to the previous discussion of voodoo death and the beliefs of primitive peoples. There we shall find objectification and the consequences of adifferentiation and other aspects of the gestalt mode of processing to be especially apparent, something that is not so easily seen in our modern, Western world where the equation of the symbol with that for which it stands is either revered as "miraculous" or simply written off as "crazy," depending on one's point of view.

The thinking and the world view of primitive natives, in contrast to our own predominantly linear world view, is influenced for the most part by the gestalt mode of processing. Therefore, in talking about what the anthropologists call "mythical thinking." I am trying to identify more clearly that which is present but not so easily seen within ourselves.

Specifically, I will discuss the primitives' *language* as well as their concepts of *time, cause,* and *identity.* I will discuss language because theirs has a predominantly gestalt quality to it as compared to the linear form of our own. Time, cause, and identity are discussed because these are the concepts by which we structure our own world view; in contrast with the prevailing gestalt quality of their language and thought, we should see a difference reflected in these concepts. Again, the purpose of discussing voodoo and primitive thinking is to see more clearly that which is present in our civilized selves but which is not so easily recognizable. The hope is that we will gain insight into just how objectification, adifferentiation, and the gestalt mode of processing affect our belief structures, our sense of reality, and our world view.

4

Primitive "Belief" and Bimodal Mental Processing

It seems reasonable to assume that both civilized and primitive individuals use a combination of "linear" and "gestalt" processing to survive and prosper in their respective worlds. However, from what has been previously said about "voodoo death," it is apparent that primitives have a world view markedly different from our own. Theirs is a world saturated with feeling, ruled by magical forces, and populated by unseen, supernatural beings. In comparing their world view with ours, the question arises as to how the differences relate to bimodal mental processing.

One might ask why this investigation is deserving of more than a curious glance. The answer is that perhaps by looking at the mentality of primitives we can better appreciate the influence of the gestalt mode of processing within ourselves. We in the West seem to be prejudiced against recognizing the legitimacy of the products of this mode of processing, products such as artistic and intuitive insights, and we seem to accord them a place somewhere behind the "more credible" position of such things as engineering and scientific truths. Perhaps this is because we do not and cannot understand the products of this gestalt processing through the medium of our own linear, sequential logic where items in the world are separate and distinct and where time, space, and causation are not blurred by feelings and desires.

Reason is used both to arrive logically at positions from observations of the world and to rationalize positions assumed for emotional reasons. Pertinent here is our less than successful attempts to recognize the effects of adifferentiation and objectification. We have not yet learned to tell the difference between the bogus rationalizations brought on by fear, hate, desire, etc., and legitimate insights that are independent of emotional prejudices and are logically consistent with observations of nature. This is an important distinction, one we must recognize if we are to understand subjective experience, for we must not be content with endorsing mysteries and ineffable "realities" as "explanations" for that which cannot be understood discursively. Certainly there are limits to our understanding, but let us not be content with the limits as they now stand.

A central issue here is whether "cause" is "natural" or "supernatural," whether events in the world and in ourselves are seen as functions of nature and therefore of "natural" causes or whether such events are "supernatural" in the sense that supernatural entities or powers "cause" them. In the latter case, these entities can be seen as symbolic, gestalt images of our own subjective life. Psychology must accept that even if the "supernatural" does exist, its mandate as a science is to begin with observations of the "natural" world and to understand them in natural terms rather than to use reason to rationalize an understanding that is consistent with super-natural assumptions. (This is not an argument against the existence of the supernatural.) Instead of assuming nonsym-bolized mysteries, can we not use reason to recognize that much of our subjective experience is not expressed in a dis-cursive, linear fashion? Instead of accepting "unknowable" realities and mysteries, can we not look rationally at our own nonrational, ineffable experience? To assume supernatural entities as "causes" is to believe that the mental images of our own emotions, feelings, desires, etc., "cause" events to happen. This is magical thinking that confuses our subjective experience with the world itself. (While there may well be reason to believe that psychokinesis does exist, I feel such phenomena will eventually be understood better in "natural" rather than "supernatural" terms.)

The concept of "cause" is one that lies within a rational scheme, for it implies the logical relationship "because A then B," and to use it for phenomena lying outside of that kind of relationship is not appropriate. (Even if "cause" involves a harmonious fit of gestalts or processes that appear to be nonlinear in function, it still fits into the linear form "because A then B.") That is, so far as "causes" exist at all, they exist within a linear mode of understanding, and to apply the concept outside of that context is a break in logic. The phrase "supernatural cause" is self-contradictory, since "cause" implies a rational and logical scheme whereas "supernatural" implies its absence. And because our own linear mode of understand-ing necessitates finding a "cause" for this situation, we conjure up "mystery" as an "explanation" for it.

To help us understand those parts of ourselves that are not rational, let us now look more carefully at the beliefs of primitives in the hope that we can learn more about those aspects of ourselves that we presently do not see very clearly, i.e., the products and influence of the gestalt mode of mental processing.

LANGUAGE

I shall first look at what Lee (1973) said about the language and world view of the natives of the Trobriand Islands, in the southwest Pacific. Whereas we might use a series of adjectives and a noun to describe something in what might be seen as a linear description, the Trobrianders' expression combines the adjectival qualities and the noun into the same word. That is, their expression lacks a linear quality and has instead a gestalt, "wholistic" quality in which multiples are gathered into a whole. In addition, we see in Lee's discussion that the natives' thinking shows (a) the absence of a concept of time and (b) the diminution of their ability to compare related items, both of which seem to be attributes that depend on one's ability to think sequentially and analytically.

> A Trobriand word refers to a self-contained concept. What we consider an attribute of a predicate, is to the Trobriander an ingredient. Where I would say, for example, "A good gardener," or "The gardener is good," the Trobriand word includes both "gardener" and "goodness"; if the gardener loses his goodness, he has lost a defining ingredient, he is something else, and he is named by means of a completely different word. A taytu (a species of yam) contains a certain degree of ripeness, bigness, roundedness, etc.; without one of these defining ingredients, it is something else, perhaps a bwanawa or a yowana. There are no adjectives in the language; the

rare words dealing with qualities are substantivized. The term "to be" does not occur; it is used neither attributively nor existentially, since existence itself is contained; it is an ingredient of being.

Events and objects are self-contained points in another respect; there is a series of beings, but no becoming. There is no temporal connection between objects. The taytu always remains itself; it does not "become" over-ripe; over-ripeness is an ingredient of another, a different thing. At some point, the taytu "turns into a yowana," which contains over-ripeness, and the "yowana," over-ripe as it is, does not put forth shoots, does not "become" a sprouting yowana. When sprouts appear, it ceases to be itself; in its place appears a selasata. Neither is there a temporal connection made . . . or, according to our own premises, perceived . . . between events; in fact, temporality is meaningless. There are no tenses, no linguistic distinctions between the past and present. There is no arrangement of activities or events into means and ends, no causal or teleologic relationships. What we consider a causal relationship in a sequence of connected events is to the Trobriander an ingredient of a patterned whole. He names this ingredient u'ula.

There is no automatic relating of any kind in the language. Except for the rarely used verbal it-differents and it-sames, there are no terms of comparison whatsoever. And we find in an analysis of behavior that the standard for behavior and of evaluation is noncomparative. (Lee, 1973, pp. 131-32)

Certainly all primitives do not think alike, so let us examine examples of primitives' thinking from various other sources to see if they also reflect the influence of a relative predominance of the gestalt mode of processing. In doing this we shall examine the concepts of (a) *time* and (b) *cause and effect,* as well as (c) *identity and separateness-of-items-and-*

events-in-the-world—concepts into which modern, civilized humans structure and organize their world views and concepts related to a linear or sequential mode of processing. In the examples to be given, we will see that time and space are not restraints to the primitives' thinking. Time itself is not discretely marked along a "time line" extending from the past, through the present, on to the future; and to whatever degree it is demarcated at all, it is done with feelings (e.g., happy or sad, etc.). And as one would expect from the gestalt mode of processing, there is in their thinking a lack of distinction and separateness in the events of the world. Instead, there is a unity of things and events that defies our civilized logic and world view. Even one's identity seems at times to merge with others or with animals and localities. As might also be expected from the gestalt mode of processing, feelings are of paramount importance: becoming personified or objectified and seen as discrete, living entities—such as witches or animals—that in turn "cause" events to happen. Instead of reason and logic being used to arrive at "natural" causes through a sequential analysis of separate and distinct events in the world, reason is used as a rationalization of and justification for feelings that have been transformed into images of supernatural entities. (This is an important point, one that I shall later show has significant consequences for the understanding of religious beliefs.)

TIME

Whereas Westerners might conceive of time as distinct and well-demarcated points on a line or "order of succession," such is not the case for primitives. Levy-Bruhl (1975) spoke of the vagueness of their concept of time, and after examining the language of primitives, he suggested that future events are not as a rule situated at any particular point on the line of futurity. (For the sake of clarity, I shall use the present tense when speaking of the primitive, knowing that such natives as described in the literature may not even exist today.) If one event is observed to follow another in a certain interval of time, primitives do in fact perceive one as being relatively future to the other, but they do not distinguish the interval between them very clearly. Furthermore, time is not valued as an object, as it is in our world; instead, it is treated with an indifference that is hard for the "civilized" mind to understand. Also, instead of distinct intervals of time being important to the primitives, they distinguish "time in a curious way, namely as happy and unhappy" (Levy-Bruhl 1978, p. 94). In other words, *feelings* seem to demarcate or distinguish time. The same author suggested that important periods of time are also characterized, not in terms of natural events but by the manifestations of the supernatural powers that occur in them. Instead of using their reasoning ability to mark off points on a time line via a linear or sequential mode of processing, primitives use their feelings, personified or objectified as supernatural entities, to characterize epochs of time.

A related point is that the thinking of the primitive is not restrained by the concept of "space." Consider, for instance, a case reported by Levy-Bruhl (1975, pp. 5–6) of an American Indian who came to a missionary and asked for some money in compensation for a pumpkin that the missionary had stolen from the Indian's garden. The missionary explained that he could not have committed the theft since he was 150 miles away at the time. For the missionary this seemed to settle the matter, and he was surprised when the Indian persisted in his claim. It turned out that the Indian had seen him steal the pumpkin, but he had seen it in a dream, the validity of which he never doubted. The missionary whom the Indian had seen in the garden and the missionary who was 150 miles away were for the Indian one and the same, and therefore, the missionary was responsible for what he had done in the dream. There were two missionaries at the same moment in two different places, and yet there was but a single missionary. For the Indian, what was considered "real" and "possible" was determined more by emotions and similarity of images than by rules of Aristotelian logic. In other words, if images can be considered to be "objectifications" of feelings, then what was real was determined by feelings instead of reason.

Another characteristic of the primitives' concept of time is the fact that past, present, and future seem to be united, or at least not separate somehow, as might be expected from the gestalt but not the linear mode of processing. For instance, Levi-Strauss (1969, p. 237), in examining the myths and ceremonies of primitive tribes, suggested that these myths and rites seemed to bring all three dimensions of time into an amalgamation in the minds of the primitives. For them there is no past, or rather, the present is merely a reliving of the past. Thus when primitives enact a religious ceremony, it is an enactment of past events, the past behaviors of ancestors, which brings the past to life. The ceremony brings the past and the present together. It is not, as our Western minds would perceive it, a matter of mimicking or remembering the past. For the primitive tribesmen, the past *is* present.

It seems apparent from these examples that the primitives' thinking is not constrained by the restrictions of space and time as these are classically used in our modern, Western experience. Instead, there is a suspension of Aristotelian logic and an equating of similar feelings or images. First comes a sense of reality and certainty as generated by our feelings, which are experienced as images via the primacy of the gestalt mode of processing; then comes the linear, discursive reasoning to justify that feeling of reality. This in a sense is similar to what was found in the experimental work with split-brain subjects described in chapter 2, where the subject said he chose the shovel because it was needed to clean out the chicken houses.

CAUSE AND EFFECT

Primitives view many things as caused by "natural" events, otherwise they cannot survive in their everyday world. But, in addition, they view events about them as also being caused by supernatural forces, which are in turn often related to malevolent feelings. Consider the case in chapter 1 of the two primitives, *S* and *K,* who went into the woods to find honey. When asked the cause of *S*'s death, the witchdoctor pronounced, and the relatives and villagers believed, that *K*'s feelings of jealousy were instrumental in the poor fellow's death. This is just one example of numerous accounts in the literature where emotions are thought to initiate events and are given supernatural status. It is not uncommon, for instance, that the death of a cow or a horse is believed to be caused by some jealous person placing the "evil eye" on the beast. For the primitive, emotions are experienced as causal agents.

Levy-Bruhl (1975) suggested that one difference between ourselves and primitives becomes apparent when something out of the ordinary happens. When there is a dramatic and emotional break in the ordinary course of natural events, primitives "sense" the presence of some supernatural force, as if *with a sudden experience of strong feelings the image or symbol of that feeling is experienced as objectively real.* They "feel" a spirit or a god or a witch in their presence and "know" or "believe" in the actual presence of such a supernatural being, which for them "causes" the otherwise unexplained event. It is as if a strong emotion "charges" a gestalt image with significance and life, and the objectification of that emotion becomes all the more alive and real. This is especially true when the stability afforded by reason has been weakened because events have happened out of the ordinary or natural sequence. Gestalt images symbolize feelings, but, at the same time, *when a feeling is intense enough it brings the symbol to conscious awareness.* That is, it appears that a particular image can be socially learned as the symbol for a feeling, as the image of a witch in some societies symbolizes fear. Thus when intense fear is experienced, that particular image is brought to mind.

Consider a report from Guinea (Levy-Bruhl 1975, pp. 21–22), where a man was attacked and killed by a shark while swimming. There were many native witnesses, but when the European investigator tried to find out what actually happened he was faced with conflicting accounts. Some said that the shark was actually not a shark at all but consisted of four or five witches who had hidden under a shark's skin. Others said that witches entered the body of a real shark and killed the poor fellow, while still others said that a witch had ordered the shark to attack. The sudden and unnatural death meant for the natives that *a witch* had *caused* the attack, the witch being an "objectification" of the unpleasant feelings generated by the swimmer's sudden death. How the witch actually brought about the death was of little consequence to the native observers. That is, concepts of cause and effect, as per the linear mode of processing, were of little importance to the natives, since for them the witch was the "cause." Said in only a slightly different way, fear was experienced as the image of a witch who was conceived as causing the event that generated the fear. *Notice a reversal of the causal sequence. Instead of events causing fear (as we might understand) along "natural" lines, when "supernatural" interpretations are involved, the fear—or rather the objectified image of the fear—causes the event.*

UNITY, SEPARATENESS, AND IDENTITY

One of the differences between the linear and the gestalt mode of processing is the fact that the former and not the latter allows for separateness, for distinctions to be made, and for the examination of relationships between items. It should be apparent from the examples already given that the primitive does not experience distinctions and separation as we do in our "civilized" minds. Consider first the unity of the personality—the self as we might say today. For the Indian who saw two missionaries in his dream, there was no difficulty in conceiving the two—one missionary in his pumpkin patch and another 150 miles away. Likewise, there was no contradiction for the natives who accused K of turning himself into a lion and eating S. Faced with the overwhelming evidence against him, even poor K ended up believing, contrary to his own previous experience, that he had turned himself into a lion and, in a fit of jealousy, had eaten his poor friend. Obviously their ideas of identity differ from ours: they see the individual as less discrete and well defined.

At this juncture let us digress and point out that the very concepts we use in our thinking are so very different from those of the primitives that there may exist a limit to our understanding. For instance, Levy-Bruhl points out that when describing primitives' beliefs in spirits and unseen forces, some investigators have used the term "soul" as if the natives' concept were similar to our own when in fact it is much different. The same thing can be said about such expressions as "family" and "marriage" and "property," but for now let us focus on the "soul."

We tend to see things as separate and distinct and thus we conceive of a body and a soul, or spirit, and then we struggle with the difficulty of trying to unite them. Such is the nature of the "mind-body" problem in Western philosophy. But for the primitive it is different. First, he has no clear-cut idea, according to Levy-Bruhl (1975, pp. 4–5), of a body and a soul, and insofar as he does conceive of a soul it is both "spiritual and material." While the linear mental processes might conceive of a separation and then try to unite the body and soul in the mind, the primitive approach seems not to see such distinctions in the first place. For both ourselves and the primitives, death means the breaking of a unity within the individual, but the natives' concept of death and separation is quite different from our own. For the primitive an individual's ghost or spirit may be found a few days after his death (a) in the grave, (b) in the neighborhood or house in which the individual lived, as well as (c) on the way to the "place of shadows." While the spirit may have broken away from the corpse, the separation is never complete; both the spirit and the corpse are believed to remain as one. It was just such a unity (lack of separation) that the Indian felt between the missionary in his dream and the one who was

150 miles away. But because of our predisposition to think in terms of separateness, we have a hard time appreciating this lack of separation, which is first and foremost *felt* by the primitive. Thus, because of our own bias, we will to some extent inevitably distort how primitives think and perceive—no matter how hard we try to empathize with them—simply because we interpret (mediate) their thought processes through a conceptual apparatus that cannot accommodate them.

The primitive feels a lack of distinction between himself and the parts of his body, such as the fragments of his hair or nail clippings. Action exerted on any one of these parts is experienced as an action upon himself as a whole, for he *is* a unity of himself and his parts. Thus the action upon a lock of hair or upon an image such as a "voodoo doll" exerts its power upon the individual himself, and it becomes more understandable why, even today, some natives object to being photographed, for this unity between themselves and their image exposes the individual to manipulation by anyone who possesses his photograph. The lack of separation experienced by the primitive applies also to his name and his possessions. The utterance of one's name can thus have an influence over the rest of his being, since he and his name are the same. Many primitives feel that whatever has been in direct contact with the individual, his clothing or weapons or cattle, *is* the individual himself. Thus, when he dies these possessions cannot belong to anyone else, for his possessions must accompany him to his new existence.

Likewise, there is a unity or lack of separation felt between the individual and his territory. With certain primitive peoples it is not permissible for a tribe to bury a stranger within their own territory. According to Loesche: "Their creeds forbid that the stranger should be buried in the locality, for in doing so they would be giving his soul a home, and who knows what it might not do?" He then goes on with the story of a Portuguese who, as a way of exception, was buried in Laugo. When there followed a period of draught the natives dug up the body and threw it into the sea, feeling that they were ridding themselves of the cause of their natural calamity.

The territory or land upon which a group of natives lives *is* the group itself. The group can never exist anywhere else and any other tribe who might try to seize the land and establish itself would be exposed to the very greatest of dangers. With many primitives there might be conflict and warfare between neighboring tribes, with many incursions of territorial rights, but conquest and annexation are not carried out since, according to Levy-Bruhl, that would expose the victor to all kinds of dangers from the "spirits" of those who had previously owned it. Each social group is not only the master of a particular local region, thereby possessing the exclusive rights of hunting and fishing, but the soil "belongs" to them. Actually, there is thought to be a unity between the primitives themselves and the soil of their locality.

There is, in addition, a unity between primitives and the animals around them. Levi-Strauss (1966) refers to the following comment by a native.

> We know what the animals do, what are the needs of the beaver, the bear, the salmon, and other creatures, because man married them and acquired the knowledge from their animal wives . . . white man has been only a short time in this country and knows very little about the animals; we have lived here thousands of years and were taught long ago by the animals themselves. The white man writes everything down in a book so that it will not be forgotten; but our ancestors

married the animals, learned all their ways, and passed on the knowledge from one generation to another. (p. 37)

Levy-Bruhl (1978) says something quite similar about the natives' relation to nature.

Their ancestors, both recent and remote, the unseen spirits and forces of all kinds, the species which people the air, water and soil, the very earth and even its rocks and incidental configurations, everything within the limits of the locality occupied by the social group "belong" to it, as we have seen, in the mystic sense of the word. (p. 385)

Whereas it is commonplace in our society to identify the individual and even to extol individuality, such is not the case for the primitive. As a single individual, he is identified as a part of his group, or rather he *is* his group in the same way that he *is* his hair clippings or clothing, etc. For instance, in some primitive societies all the members of the family are equally responsible for the death of any one of them. Our "civilized" way of saying all this is that an individual is first a member of his group, but this is not quite accurate. In emphasizing this point, Levy-Bruhl (1978) quotes Jocotte.

As a rule among the Bafutof, the important facts of life are not left to individual caprice, but regulated and arranged by the entire family. In short, the individual never really attains his majority; he must be more or less in a tutelage of his family, clan, and tribe. He has no individuality; he is but a member of the final or national community. (p. 400)

The early missionaries to these primitive societies were confronted with this problem and it was particularly puzzling to them, for they were interested in saving the individual souls.

> Nobody wants to make up his mind on his own account. The councils of the old men must decide in cases of the change in religion . . . it would be all or none . . . the strictness of the social bond relieves the individual of all responsibility, but at the same time, it deprives him of his personal liberty. (Levy-Bruhl 1978, p. 400)

FEELINGS AND THE SENSE OF REALITY

It is clear that the primitives' experience of the world is richly colored with emotions and feelings. They *feel* unseen forces and they *sense* the presence of an unseen world of spirits and supernatural entities. They sense and feel a oneness with others and with the environment, and they *feel* a sense of reality. Whereas today we might emphasize the cognitive aspects of a belief and might speak of "a belief system" as a codified set of pronouncements, for the primitive native, "belief" is more a *sense* or a *feeling* of reality.

We have seen how the linear, analytic mode of mental processing is suited for making distinctions, for the expression of the logic of mathematics and discursive reason, and for the propositional form of language. We suggest that one component of our sense of reality is a product of this mode of mental processing, a component that is characterized by discretely separated items in the world structured by the linear notions of time and cause. A second component of our sense of reality comes from our gestalt, synthetic, wholistic mode of processing that is well suited for the formation of visual and auditory images and for the symbolic expression of emotions. We have suggested that in the primitives' experience, feelings become objectified and symbolized as images that are felt as "real," such as the image of a witch (that in turn may take the form of a lion or a shark). In such a case, the image itself symbolizes a constellation of ideas or emotions which are brought together in a synthetic or gestalt integration into the single image. The visual image of a witch, the name of the witch, or the word *witch* itself serves as a symbol for the ideas and the emotions. For the primitive the image or idea of a witch has all the power and significance of the witch itself. The symbol and the "thing" for which the symbol stands are one. When an emotion-laden event interrupts the usual course of events, the emotions so experienced are felt as the presence of supernatural entities; the feelings are symbolically experienced and objectified in the mind of the native as the experience of a witch or some other supernatural entity. These in turn are considered to be the cause of the events in question. In this formulation the strong emotional experience at a sudden and unexpected death would, for instance, be construed as the cause of the individual's demise.

The purpose of examining in detail the concepts of time, cause, identity, and the importance of feelings in the primitives' sense of reality is to help us identify these same phenomena within ourselves. At the same time, this examination of the primitives' beliefs allows us a new way of understanding magical and superstitious beliefs. The gestalt mode creates images that symbolize feelings, and, because of the gestalt quality of primitive languages, we can speculate that feelings are important in their thinking and in their world view. Thus we find time, cause, and identity being related through feelings rather than in a more linear or logical manner. Indeed, strong emotions are symbolized for the primitive as supernatural entities and powers, and reason conceives of these powers as causing events in the world. That is, reason does not so much arrive at logical positions derived from observations of the world but rationalizes magical and superstitious "causes." With the relative predominance of the gestalt mode, feelings determine the "cause," establish the "identity," and relate events to one another regardless of spatial or temporal considerations. In the next chapter, I shall suggest some implications that this holds for psychology, religion, and philosophy.

5

Some Implications

Thus far, I have argued that we have experimental grounding in the scientific world of "fact" for the claim that the human mind processes experiences in two distinctly different modes, the linear and the gestalt, which correlate generally with the left and the right cerebral hemispheres respectively. Furthermore, I have shown that the gestalt mode is involved in the formation of symbolic images while the linear mode is concerned with an appreciation of relationships *between* these symbols. I have also tried to show that a predominance of one or the other of these modes in one's thinking and believing leads to two entirely different ways of expressing experience, the one leading to artistic and religious expression and to a world view rich in feelings, while the other leads to an expression of experience in a more analytic and structured form.

Much energy has thus far been spent exploring the thinking and the beliefs of primitives; I dwelled particularly on their language and their concepts of time, cause, and identity.

Primitive language was focused upon because it has a decidedly gestalt quality about it, unlike our own, which is primarily influenced by the linear mode of mental processing. I focused on time, cause, and identity because these are concepts by which modern, Western individuals structure not only their world view but their sense of reality. In doing so we arrived at insightful differences between the primitive world of magic and the world of modern science. This investigation allowed us to understand magic and superstition as the products of belief systems in which feelings, objectified as supernatural powers via the gestalt mode, cause events to happen. As our discussion proceeds, we shall see that these objectified feelings have implications for religion per se, but the primary purpose in exploring the beliefs of primitives is to help us recognize something not so easily seen within ourselves, namely, the influence of the gestalt mode of mental processing. While there is some resistance to the idea, we in the West must admit that believing is more than a rational experience and that it also involves such elements as emotions, intentions, desires, and values.

Earlier it was suggested that the combination of these ideas about bimodal mental processing and symbolism could generate new ideas and thus, to paraphrase Langer, be a "generative hybrid" of ideas. If so, just what are the implications of what we have been saying? Does it have any practical or theoretical implications? Is the idea of bimodal mental processing combined with ideas about the symbolic process really a new generative hybrid of ideas that can serve to inspire a new wave of creative ideas? I think it is. In the following discussion of some possible implications of this hybrid, I shall briefly and albeit superficially mention some items, for the purpose here is to glance at a larger image within which these ideas rest. Certainly the implications mentioned are not fully developed at this point, for the purpose is to develop a more global perspective rather than emphasizing precision.

SOME POSSIBLE IMPLICATIONS FOR PSYCHOTHERAPY

From a practical point of view, we can see in psychotherapy patients blatant evidence of the gestalt mode of processing. For instance, while I was writing this chapter I saw a thirty-five-year-old professional woman, Mary D., who had, during the week since her last therapy session, burned me in effigy. A remark I had made the previous week had led Mary to feel that she and I were "fused," that she could not tell us apart. This scared her, and she felt that she had to kill me in order to free herself. Mary had had a habit, unbeknown to me, of taking a tissue each week as she left my office to use as a magical amulet to ward off the evil personalities in her mind. She took these tissues, along with various bills and receipts I had given her, put them in a clay pot and burned them, believing that in doing so she had killed me. This act was not intended to have some metaphorical meaning; she genuinely thought of me as a pile of charred bones and ashes. Not long afterward, Mary was brought to my office in a confused state. So amazed was she at seeing me that she had to touch me to believe that I was alive and real; several days later she came by my office unannounced to reassure herself that I was indeed alive.

The interesting thing is that Mary and I had never discussed voodoo or burning in effigy, and it is as if she reached back into some primordial part of herself to find a way of

ridding herself of her feelings and attachments to me. Be
that as it may, this woman's magical thinking presents a clear
example of someone functioning primarily in the gestalt mode
of processing: by destroying these symbols of me and our
relationship, she did indeed free herself to some extent from
her attachment to me and to therapy. She did, however, have
to pay the price of being confused as her reason and the
linear mode of processing receded.

Another demonstration of the influence of the gestalt mode
of processing as it pertains to magical thinking is expressed
in the following words taken from a therapy session with
a patient, Carol A.

> She (her little daughter) had to have a cystogram. . . . I felt
> like I wanted to do it for her, like I wanted to protect her
> from it. And that kind of paved the way to my making it
> not so bad for her. I tried to go through the whole thing
> mentally and recite exactly how it would be and how much
> it would hurt and what if this and what if that happened.
> I kind of pictured it in my mind, and I got myself all worked
> up over it as a way of protecting her.

Is this quotation from a primitive native mother of a
century ago who believed in a magical, mental ritual for pro-
tecting her daughter? Obviously the reference to a cystogram
suggests not, and we shall see in the next few paragraphs
further quotations of her thoughts that are strikingly similar
to the previously reported accounts of the beliefs of primitives.
Our purpose here in referring to material taken from therapy
sessions with psychiatric patients is twofold. First, it is yet
another source of corroborative evidence for the existence
of bimodal mental processing. Admittedly, by itself it is not

strong evidence, but its similarity to the previous accounts of primitives supports the validity of the concept of bimodal mental processing. In addition, it brings the whole discussion closer to home, closer to an appreciation of just how bimodal mental processing manifests itself in our everyday life and how it can lead to a practical understanding of psychologically disturbed patients.

Because these are psychiatric patients, it might be argued that we cannot draw conclusions about "normal" mental functioning from such a source. However, even though Carol— a twenty-eight-year-old woman who had been in therapy several years because of severe anxiety, bulimia, and depression —was, to be sure, psychologically crippled, I would suggest that the magical thinking she struggled against is more prevalent in the general population today than most of us would like to admit. Furthermore, her primary reason for seeing a psychiatrist was to extricate herself from a rather sick belief system endemic in her family and community. But let us go on to further explore Carol's thoughts. They reflect a belief in magical powers and an inability to separate and discriminate, both of which are similar to those of primitives whose thinking and beliefs have a decidedly gestalt quality. Thus she continued in her description of how she and her family reacted to death and illness.

> Any time my mother has been sick I can't rest. I feel like she is lying there in pain and I should be in pain. Or like if I go home from the hospital I get afraid that she is going to die when I am gone. . . . I feel that I just have to be worried, that I have to be thinking about what she is going through. And if I don't, I just feel that something bad will happen.
>
> Or I feel that when she has some type of sickness . . . or

operation that I want to really do it for her. I start dreading it and actually get physically sick, and I'm afraid not to do that. Then I just worry about every time that I was angry with her or had bad feelings towards her.

When he (her father) got sick, she (her mother) just said he'd get better if we all believed. He had lung cancer, and they (the doctors) thought he had cancer in other places. . . . I felt at that point I had a lot to do with it. I felt that I should pray about it all the time and really believe. He was real sick, spitting up blood, and she kept praying, and people in the family kept saying "If you just believe everything would be fine." And so I tried to do that. But I guess I felt guilty, and I was afraid I was contributing to his not getting well by thinking negative about it.

Well, they (her family and relatives). . . like to sit around and drink coffee, and they talk at the table . . . (and) . . . say that people get what they deserve. If something happens to someone's children, they'll say, "Well, if they really appreciated those children and were grateful, then that wouldn't have happened." Like if something happens to somebody's spouse and the other person happens to be a bad person, they'll say that somehow that's how it works out, that God was probably punishing the bad person by letting the person die, and that the person that's alive is going to be grieved and get what he deserves.

I was always taught "to think bad" was as bad as to do it. That's what I've heard my mother, her sister, and her mother, my grandmother, say. I've heard this over and over. "If you're gonna think it, you might as well do it. That's just as bad." I always feel guilty about having the thought that I hated her (her mother), that I had hurt her by thinking that I hated her. . . . I was even afraid to think it. If I was angry, just in my room, I would think that God knows about this and there's no privacy even in your room because He knows if you're angry and if you hate somebody. Somehow it's still gonna touch them. It's still gonna make them feel bad. I felt like I would be punished for being bad, that I was being bad and that I would be punished. But I felt that somehow it would hurt my mother, that He (God) would see what I felt about my mother and then hurt her.

(And when her mother was sick,) the doctors told her not to smoke, not to do this and that and to do these certain things. And maybe if she does that it would help her live longer, and it makes a lot of sense. But yet she sends so much money to . . . (a well known evangelist) . . . and she feels that she's covered. She goes around saying, "Well, I believe in God and I'm not sick," and then she smokes and drinks coffee and does whatever she wants.

(And she was pregnant.) The doctor told me yesterday that the baby might be coming early and to stay in bed a lot. I listened and I immediately thought "I've been having all these feelings, just wanting this baby out of my body. I'm so tired of this." I felt that God was punishing me for having these thoughts of being tired of carrying the baby, for not being sure that I want it.

In the above quote from Carol's therapy session, we witness thought processes that are consistent with a primitive, uncivilized mind. There is magical thinking about supernatural entities and powers. A mother can "protect" her daughter from pain and unforeseen complications by the prior mental imaging of a surgical procedure. A young woman can protect her mother by remaining in close proximity or hurt her by leaving. She can protect her father from advanced cancer through "believing" in the right way, or hurt his chances of survival by not doing so. (Perhaps "believing" in a certain way may have beneficial or detrimental physiological consequences; that is not the issue here. What is at issue is the causative agent, whether it is a supernatural entity, as the natives and this woman's family might maintain, or whether it is understood in a more "naturalistic" line as the product of a unique physiological or psychological state.) Here, as in the case of primitive beliefs, we see that thoughts and "feelings" can harm others. We previously saw how the jealousy of a young primitive could "cause" a comrade to be torn to bits by a lion, and in this instance we see that a daughter's resentment can "harm" her mother or her own unborn child. (Again, the issue is not whether one's emotional state can affect one's unborn child. It is, instead, whether or not supernatural entities are involved.) And as a native might make offerings to sway the influence of the gods, here we find a mother trying to bribe God by giving money to his presumed envoy, hoping to protect her health even if she ignored the doctor's advice. Just as a primitive might be apprehensive of the wrath of his god, so we see in this patient and her family the fear that God would punish someone for having "bad thoughts" or even punish one's children or spouse for having lived a "bad life."

The unity and lack of separateness discussed in chapter 4 as characteristic of the primitive's existence could be seen particularly in this young woman. She was crippled by her belief that feelings and thoughts affect events and persons at a distance; she was equally crippled by her inability to separate her own identity, thoughts, and feelings from those of her family. She experienced severe anxiety concerning the harm she might do by thinking or feeling the wrong thing, and she felt guilt for having already done so.

In primitive societies there is a unity or collectiveness among the tribal and family members, and so in this patient's family there is a similar lack of separation. There is the belief that each family member's feelings affect the other, as Carol A.'s feeling of anger affected her mother and her mother's reaction affected Carol herself. This interaction of feeling affected the other family members who might witness it. And just as each tribal member reinforced the magical thinking of the others, so in this case the individual family members reinforced one another's magical beliefs. The collectiveness of her family's belief system entrapped Carol and necessitated her therapy. When she tried to extricate herself from its network, it hindered her separation from the group and her growth as an individual.

One usual explanation for the phenomena just described is that these beliefs are "learned" by the patient, modeled after repeatedly witnessing similar experiences within the family circle. Here an additional factor can be suggested. I propose that it also reflects the basic limitation of the gestalt mode of processing, its inability to allow for discriminations and separateness. Furthermore, Carol has a belief system in which the concepts of cause, time, and identity are more predominantly influenced by the gestalt mode of processing. The thesis is this: with matters that elicit strong emotional responses—for example, death and illness—there is a relative lack of influence of the linear mode of processing and a relative predominance of influence of the gestalt mode. When Carol and her family discussed cancer and health matters or other subjects that elicited fear or anger, they experienced an increased inability to discriminate and separate their own identity, thoughts, and feelings from the others in the group.

On what basis do I make these suggestions? Levy-Bruhl commented that primitive tribesmen thought along naturalistic lines of cause and effect until something out of the ordinary happened that was emotionally stimulating. For instance, if a native was killed by a shark while swimming or attacked by a lion while in the woods alone (events that induce strong and violent feelings), then the natural cause-and-effect of their normal, everyday world was seemingly replaced by the causal influence of supernatural powers and entities. When that occurred, a whole new perspective was generated in which the reasoned view of the world receded and emotions assumed paramount importance, especially emotions symbolized by images of supernatural beings.

In the following quotation taken from a therapy session, Carol graphically describes how she felt and thought when dealing with matters that brought forth strong emotions.

> It's like I'm two different people. It's like I feel like two different people. One person functions and thinks a certain way, and then when anything happens, whenever I have a problem, a crisis comes up or something like this, I'm just all feelings. I can't think. I get confused. I feel real confused.

Carol described herself as functioning in two separate ways, depending on how emotionally upset she was. As long as she was calm and undisturbed, she thought quite logically and rationally, but when she became emotionally upset it was as if another part of herself took over. Her reason was effected, and she felt confused as her rational self receded and her beliefs and actions seemed to ensue primarily from her emotions. This phenomena is essentially of the same order as that of the primitive whose friend was killed by a shark or torn apart by a lion. In such cases the influence of reason retreated into the background, and their behaviors and beliefs flowed from their feelings. When their emotions reached a certain intensity, it seems that their sense of reality was determined by feelings rather than by logic and reason.

Another patient, a thirty-one-year-old male named Ralph B., presented a history suggesting the same phenomenon. He was a college graduate who had for many years been subject to very severe anxiety and panic attacks, for which he had been seeing a therapist for four to five years before coming to see me on the recommendation of a relative whom I had successfully treated. Ralph was handicapped by his anxiety and its resulting lack of confidence, which cost him many extra years in college. Having been raised by parents who were extraordinarily critical and intolerant of his independent thinking, Ralph had learned to accept what they said as gospel. He never questioned their judgment, even though he was thirty-one years of age by the time he entered therapy.

On the day in question, Ralph came into my office and began to talk about the fact that he felt he was going to die. This had happened in previous sessions, but on this occasion he said that it would be God's judgment that he was to die, and this made him exceedingly anxious. During the previous week, Ralph had spoken with a girl who suggested they read the Bible, and in it they found references to devils and demons. Determined to change his life, Ralph resolved never to smoke again and was convinced that if he were to do so it would only be because of the corrupting influence of a devil or demon within him.

In spite of his resolve, it was not long before Ralph began to smoke, and he immediately felt the presence and influence of a demon. To calm himself he went for a walk, but as he proceeded he felt the demon's influence growing. Fearful that the demon would possess and control him entirely, he panicked and became frightened to the point of running for several hours through the night. He finally forced himself to concentrate on events around him—the noises and behavior of passers-by—and he gradually became more calm.

As Ralph began to talk in therapy about what had happened, he experienced a confusion similar to Carol's; the influence of reason receded and emotions determined his behavior and beliefs. As he started to relate his experience, Ralph began to sweat and soon became extremely anxious, feeling somewhat confused as if he was "out in space." Again, he wanted to die; he spoke of it as being "God's judgment" that he die since he had done bad things, including his smoking.

This particular patient demonstrated a relationship between his anxiety on the one hand and his tendency to have his "natural world" invaded by a different set of laws, where feelings can cause things to happen and where supernatural beings emit their awesome powers. It seems quite clear that as Ralph's "natural" world view—one structured by reason and logic—receded into the background and the emotionally laden demonic belief grew in influence, he felt a threat to the integrity of his own being. It seems as if his own integrated sense of self was threatened; the decreased influence of logic—the linear mode of processing—and the increased influence of emotions and symbolic images seemed to loosen the integrity of the "ego," his sense of self.

After listening to Ralph describe his feelings, I suggested that in fact he was probably not so important that God really cared about his living or dying, that perhaps God had ordained certain general laws of nature to determine these sorts of things. It was my suspicion that God would rather let natural events take place than to interfere with such laws just to kill him.

With this observation Ralph felt better, but he did feel

a sense of anxiety for having said what he did. He had never told anyone about feeling that he was going to die by God's judgment, and he suspected that this disclosure might make him appear stupid or crazy. He felt bad because he thought perhaps I (his therapist) would think less of him. At one point he blurted out: "Oh, please forgive me. Don't let me say this." He was concerned that what he was saying was crazy, and he wanted me to not let him appear crazy. Ralph wanted me to play the part of an omnipotent being (a) whose judgment he feared, (b) who could forgive him, and (c) who at the same time could control him so as not to let him say or do certain things. In essence he wanted me to be a god-like figure and to assume responsibility for his actions and feelings, a theme that was reflected in his demonic belief as well.

As in the case of the primitives, the image of a demon was already established within Ralph's belief system as a symbol for malevolent and evil powers. At the same time, he had a lifelong history of feeling that he was "bad," in addition to his anxiety, which had its roots in a very critical, angry, and overbearing father and a weak but belittling mother. Ralph's personal experience of fear and his feeling that he was "bad" became fused with the cultural image of the demon or devil, which also induced these feelings. The feelings were the same, and so the culturally learned image expressed the personal experience.

At this point an intriguing development occurred; in Ralph's mind the image of a demon became the symbol for a variety of conflicting themes. It symbolized his own tendency to criticize and punish himself as well as his fear of being punished. It also symbolized the personal source of his tribulations, namely his father, as well as the culturally learned source of his "badness" and the cause of his fear. This condensation of so many elements into one whole is characteristic of the gestalt mode of mental processing. In this case it synthesized the entire "experiential gestalt," the experience of both the subjective world and the objective world, into a single whole, into one undifferentiated experience. In other words, *the symbol represented the totality of the experience, the "inside" feelings and the "outside" cause (both the father and the demon).* The "inside" feelings included both his anger at himself for having smoked and the fear of being punished, and as such the demon symbolically represented both sides of a conflict. The symbol of a demon "linked" all of this, so that the entirety of the experience was "contained" in the symbol, as it were.

An additional point is that the image of a demon relieved Ralph of responsibility for his own unacceptable desires, feelings, and behaviors. The "evil" feelings of being "bad" and the angry, punitive tendency to punish were both exteriorized and experienced as an outside influence, symbolized by the image of the demon. As such it relieved him of any personal responsibility for both wanting to smoke and wanting to punish himself for having smoked. The symbol of a demon could, in a sense, be seen as Ralph's way of removing himself from both the responsibility for having smoked and the conflict that this generated.

In summary, for Ralph the demon represented the condensation of a number of different experiences into one symbolic focal point, a characteristic of the gestalt mode of processing. It represented (a) the "inside" feelings which in themselves represented both sides of a conflict; (b) the "outside" cause that included both the culturally determined image of the demon and the patient's personal experience with his father*; and (c) at the same time, because it was objectified and seen as outside of himself, it relieved the patient of personal responsibility for his feelings and actions. After all, "The devil made me do it." This combination of so many elements into a single whole is characteristic of the gestalt mode.

Besides the more practical issues that are raised for psychotherapy, there are implications of a more theoretical nature as well. Let me mention a few without trying to elaborate on them at this point.

IMPLICATIONS FOR PSYCHIATRY AND PSYCHOLOGY

From a psychological or psychotherapeutic point of view, the patients' lack of ability to discriminate and separate (evidenced in primitive world views) presents itself in their lives in the form of problems having to do (it would seem) with separation and individuation. The discussion here is obviously related to gestalt psychology, for these ideas can be viewed as an extension of that theory. We have, for instance, borrowed from their ideas in suggesting that the inability to discriminate and to separate, which is associated with the gestalt mode of processing, is a variation of the observation in gestalt psychiatry that there is a diminution of an awareness of the parts when one's attention is focused on the whole gestalt.

The theory of cognitive dissonance, which also shares historical roots with Gestalt psychology, can be integrated within the body of this thesis, for it focuses on the combination

---

*The important question is here being ignored as to whether the image of a demon or devil is inherent as a species-specific archetype and thus more than a "culturally" determined image.

of various cognitive functions, a process that theoretically applies to the integration of these two modes. By recognizing the importance of responsibility and the choice that goes along with cognitive dissonance theory, we can incorporate these existential issues into our thesis, something that has important implications for psychotherapy. (This will be discussed further in chapter 8.)

Although it has yet to be discussed, work from the split-brain experiments suggests a unique relationship between language, the linear mode of processing, and what we might call conscious awareness, as well as a special relationship between unconscious mental processes and the gestalt mode. Galin (1974) specifically examined the implications that cerebral specialization has for psychiatry and noted the parallel between "the functioning of the isolated right hemisphere and mental processes that are repressed, unconscious, and unable to directly control behavior" (p. 581). He saw conversion reactions, for example, as being manifestations of the "right-brain" (gestalt) type of mental processing, and he speculated that at least some instances of repression can be understood in terms of mental events in the right hemisphere becoming functionally disconnected from the left through inhibition of neuron transmission across the corpus callosum. In such a case "we might expect that unconscious ideation would be expressed primarily through channels that are not preempted by the dominant verbal left hemisphere" (p. 581).

Galin further suggested that cerebral specialization might help us understand such phenomena as autonomic asymmetries, hemispheric differences in coping strategies, and affective reactions such as "la belle indifference" and the "catastrophic response," possible differences in therapeutic responses to left and right hemispheres during administration of electroconvulsive shock treatments, and various responses to field-dependency testing, all rather significant to psychology and psychiatry.

Since Galin expressed these thoughts, experts in the field, including Galin himself (1988), have moved away from a simple left/right dichotomy in understanding the correlation of psychological experiences with anatomical features of the brain. It is now recognized that the concept of *regional* brain dysfunction makes perhaps more sense than hemispheric dysfunction, with "regional" including *intra*hemispheric regions and "dysfunction" including gradient changes or balances between various areas, such as anterior/posterior, medial/lateral, and subcortical/cortical regions. Indeed, the picture seems ever so much more complicated now than it appeared even a decade ago; but however the anatomical considerations are eventually settled, the linear/gestalt distinction seems to hold true on the psychological plane. Analysis is needed on several levels: anatomical, biochemical, physiological, as well as psychological. It is the latter with which we are now concerned. It is hoped that the controversies concerning the other levels of analysis will not contaminate the psychological, thereby discouraging us from using the linear/gestalt distinction. And it is further hoped that these various levels of thought can eventually be correlated so that the future might promise an integration of neurological, physiological, biochemical, and psychological phenomena, but such is not the case for now.

If psychotherapy consists of "making conscious that which was unconscious," as Freud and so many others have suggested, then what has just been mentioned about the relationship between the two modes of processing and consciousness and unconsciousness relates to psychotherapy in the most intimate way.

Since the images in our nightly dreams serve as gestalt images, we can understand that because of adifferentiation—the inability to distinguish the symbol from that for which it stands—the dream elements *are* our emotions, values, and subjective experiences. We can understand that because of the lack of ability to separate or to make distinctions (characteristic of the gestalt mode), we find in dreams the condensation of several images into a single element: the part standing for the whole and the absence of time as an ordering principle, which were identified in primitive thinking as characteristic of the gestalt mode of processing. Furthermore, in dreams, just as in primitive thinking, we find a special relationship between emotions and gestalt symbols. Emotions and "wishes," for instance, "cause" events to happen. All of these are of course classical psychoanalytic formulations and thus represent a correlation between unconscious processes and the beliefs of primitives as well as a concurrence between Freud and the philosophers Cassirer and Langer, who spoke of symbolism and symbolic forms, which in turn represents a concurrence of Freud, Cassirer, Langer, and split-brain research.

Psychoanalytic formulations about object relations seem also to be related to what we have called "experiential gestalts" as well as adifferentiation. The latter could be seen as an inability of the person to differentiate his own internalized image of an outside object from his subjective meaning for that object. That seems only one step removed from the infant's inability to distinguish himself from his mother's nipple, his inability to differentiate self from world, which Kernberg, for instance, suggests is one of the main tasks confronting infants. Exactly how all this is related remains to be clarified, but they are in the same ballpark. Perhaps psychoanalysis and neurology will eventually be reconciled, as Freud intended in the first place.

IMPLICATIONS FOR PHILOSOPHY

In philosophy there are implications for what we call the mind-body problem. As has already been suggested, where the gestalt mode predominantly influences one's thinking there *is* no problem because there *is no separation* of what our Western, linear minds call the mind and the body. However, questions of an epistemological nature do arise. Is it the case that knowledge is obtained only by logic, which of course would limit us to what can be expressed in a linear form, or does the gestalt mode also lead to "knowledge"?

If questions emerge about how we come to know things, it is only a matter of time before inquiries commence concerning what can be known—what is real. In addition, there is the further investigation into the relationship between what actually is real and what is "felt" or perceived to be real.

Descartes (1958) set a precedent with his emphasis on reason and logic, and Kant (1896) described his categories of pure reason. What they had to say has helped to guide Western thought since the seventeenth century. But from this perspective, what they and most of the philosophers since that time have had to say is limited to experience that can be expressed in a linear form, leaving unexplored a whole area of our experience that does not lend itself to that form of expression. The outstanding exception to the rationalist view is what Cassirer said about there being other symbolic forms than reason and logic per se.

What Cassirer and Langer have had to say on this subject deserves more attention from the philosophical community. They both maintained that there are other *forms* of experience (experiencing) besides language and its discursive symbolism, forms such as music and the visual arts, which are known through gestalt symbols. When one paints a picture or sculpts a statue one is transforming experience into symbolic form. Likewise, when one writes or plays music one creates form, form expressing feeling and subjective experience. Even action, such as the religious dancing of primitive peoples, can be seen as transforming experience into form. All of these forms legitimately convey meaning in that they symbolize or "stand for" experience. A painting, for instance, has contextual meaning in that it lies in its matrix of connotations: the feelings, values, etc., associated with it. Perhaps such forms lack the capacity for analytic precision and logic characteristic of mathematics and language, but they have a meaning that is richly imbued with feeling to a degree that is lacking in discursive symbolism.

A theory of mind that limits understanding to its discursive form rules out, for instance, visual forms from the domain of understanding and meaning. We experience nature through our senses and those forms and qualities that we distinguish, recognize, remember, and imagine also function as gestalt symbols that convey meaning.

In esthetics we can see that when an artist produces a work of art it is his attempt to materialize those gestalt, symbolic images of his imagination, gestalt images that have emotional and value-laden significance. Because words can function as gestalt images, when they are used in poetry, which is basically arranged in a linear way, the poetic is able to bring us back and forth from the linear to the gestalt modes of experiencing symbols, where certain images have particular impact because they function as gestalt symbols with several different connotative meanings.

It only makes sense that the human mind functions as a coordinated interplay between these two modes of processing, and it seems conceivable that creativity may be seen as a product of the mind's interplay between these two modes of processing.

For philosophy of culture the bimodal view has implications in that, as Northrop has pointed out, our Western cultures emphasize the linear mode of processing while the Eastern cultures generally emphasize the gestalt form.

IMPLICATIONS FOR UNDERSTANDING MAGICAL BELIEFS

Perhaps one of the most interesting implications of these ideas is that they may shed new light on the relationship between science and magic, one that can best be understood as confrontational and based on two fundamentally different modes of mental processing. Thus antagonism can be summed up as a clash between different and incompatible notions of time, cause, and identity, as well as two entirely different world views and senses of reality.

Years ago, James suggested that the various religions differed in their "overbeliefs," in their particular rational understanding of religious experience, and in their rationalizations of what he considered "invasions" from the unconscious. To put this in the correct perspective, let us first consider how scientific belief and magical belief differ in their respective use of reason. Science starts from observations of nature (including human beings) and includes these observations within a reasoned gestalt of understanding. Just exactly how this applies to subjective experience can best be examined by seeing how it differs from magical beliefs.

It is not reason per se that differentiates the two, for

both magical beliefs and science include reason in their formulations. They differ with regard to how feelings influence their formulations and what each considers an initial cause. That is, they differ in what they consider to be the fundamental facts from which to start their respective lines of reasoning. Science starts with observations of nature, with a "natural" point of reference while magical belief rests its reason on supernatural "facts."

This difference in the lines of reasoning emanating from an initial natural cause versus an initial supernatural cause is more clearly demonstrated in an examination of how the two would approach the same event. Consider the previously reported case vignette of a native being killed by a shark while swimming. The natural perspective assumes that the man was a victim of his swimming in an area where a shark happened to be feeding. If one wanted to investigate further, one would look into the feeding habits of sharks, the food supply available at the time, the climatic conditions, the water conditions, and so forth. From a natural perspective, "cause" is related to a preceding event in a natural flow of events within nature itself. However, the supernatural thought of the primitives included causes related to supernatural powers and entities, for in their minds it was reasoned that a *witch* killed the poor fellow. The frightening death of a comrade brought the culturally learned image of a witch to mind (to life), and the witch was seen as *the cause* of death. The natural perspective is that the death "caused" the fear. The supernatural perspective is that the witch (who is the symbolic image of the fear) caused the event.

Note the reversal of logic here: from the natural view, the event caused the fear, while from the supernatural perspective, the fear (or rather the symbolic image of the fear) caused the event. In either case, reason forms a causal chain of events, but in the supernatural perspective the gestalt image (the objectification) of the feeling is the initial cause, while in the natural view a natural event initiates the causal sequence. Reason is present in both instances, and the difference between the "natural" and the "supernatural" view is in the initial cause from which the reasoning starts. In one case it is a natural event, and in the other it is (from a natural perspective) the symbolic image of a subjective experience.

In the natural (scientific) world view, symbols are points in an endless series or line of events, while in the magical or supernatural perspective, they can become animated and as such can be seen as causative agents in the world. This difference becomes problematic when especially intense feelings are experienced. On such occasions the fact that the image symbolizes feelings overshadows its linear function, and the image, be it sensory or purely ideational, seems to be invested with feelings and thus felt to be alive and in the objective world. In such a case, because of the predominance of the gestalt mode and the absence of the linear mode, there is no differentiation between the image and the feeling it symbolizes (adifferentiation). If the former is a sensory image of an object in the world, such as a tree or a rock, then that tree or rock is felt to be alive, as if it is invested with a spirit or "holiness," and such objects have been considered sacred or holy throughout religious history. If, however, the image is not sensory, such as the idea of a witch, then that ideational image is also felt to be alive and in the world of objective reality, even though there is no apparent sensory referent. (The human mind will, however, search for an object to use as a symbol. Thus we had the killing of "witches" until very recently.) The (culturally learned) idea of a witch is then felt to be objectively real when feelings associated with it, such as fear or anxiety, are intensely experienced. In this way a feeling or an idea is objectified (felt to be in the objective as opposed to the subjective experiential world), something perhaps more easily seen in primitives' experiences of "the sacred." (But to be consistent, one must admit that [in Otto's words] even in the more "evolved" or mature religions the same phenomenon exists. The "devil" and "God" are, from this perspective, objectifications of elements within ourselves.)

These ideas allow us to see that in the magical use of effigies, for instance, the magical power exerts its influence because of the mind's inability to differentiate the symbol from that for which it stands. Sticking a pin into a voodoo doll is the same as doing it to the person himself, and burning one's therapist in effigy is the same as burning him in person.

The importance of language in magical belief is brought to the forefront, for we have seen that when a language is more gestalt and less linear it is better suited for feelings to enter into concepts of time, space, cause, and identity. Whereas the linear mode adds structure to these concepts and therefore to a world view, when the gestalt mode predominates in language, as it does in that of the Trobriand Islanders, these concepts as well as one's sense of reality become more fluid and more influenced by feelings.

IMPLICATIONS FOR RELIGION

Perhaps the most obvious implication is that these ideas bear upon the concept of "believing," a central theme in religion, and to the relationship between reason and faith—between believing that is based primarily on experience that can be expressed in a linear form and that which cannot.

An interesting possibility emerges in that the ideas presented here might conceivably help us understand the conflicts between those individuals who may have a more literal interpretation of Scripture and those who have a more liberal interpretation, since the former might be seen as more prone to objectification and less toward separating the symbol from that for which it stands.

An appreciation of the lack of separation, characteristic of the gestalt mode, helps us better understand religious ritual. It is more than the act of mimicking or remembering past ceremonies; it is an act that *brings the past and the present together.* The past *is* present because where one's thinking is predominantly influenced by the gestalt mode of processing, time is lacking as a structuring principle.

The gestalt mode's characteristic lack of separation has implications for the history of organized religion as well. It can be shown that every great religion goes through a crisis in its historical evolution where the symbol is recognized as different from that for which the symbol stands. At such times the religious leaders overcome adifferentiation and recognize that an idol, for instance, only "stands for" God and is not to be worshiped in itself. (This will be discussed in chapter 6.)

This question of seeing the difference between the symbol and that for which it stands is just the kind of controversy that surrounds the question of transubstantiation. In other words, in the ritual of Holy Communion, do the bread and the wine actually change into the body and blood of Christ or do they only "stand for" the latter? Are the bread and wine "only symbols" or is there an actual mystical experience of unity with the body of Christ?

Furthermore, this fusing of emotions with an image allows us to look afresh at a classical religious experience, namely, that of "the sacred." When a native experiences a place as Holy or Taboo, he combines or fuses his own feelings with his experience of the world itself. His own subjective feelings and his image of the world are experienced as one, an action characteristic of the gestalt mode of processing. And if such an experience of "the sacred" can be seen as the *sine qua non* of religion, as some religious scholars have maintained, then this perspective allows us to look psychologically and perhaps even neurologically at religious experience in an important new way.

Additionally, one would say that the age-old conflict between science and religion might be viewed in the light of a conflict between two modes of mental processing that lie within the psychological depths of each of us. Certainly science is not so free of subjective experience as it was once thought, for authors such as Polanyi and Kuhn have correctly called that into question. But to conclude that science and religion are equally subjective is certainly wrong, or at least it would be wrong to say they are subjective in the same way. Cassirer maintained that religion is one form through which the human mind symbolically expresses itself, and in light of the present discussion it could be said that in doing so the feelings and emotions thus expressed are most easily symbolized via gestalt images. In the same spirit science can be said to be another form that the human mind uses to express itself, except that in this case its capacity to symbolize logical relationships to meet scientific ends is most easily expressed via the linear mode.

In this first part of my investigation I have sought to explore some implications that split-brain research and bimodal mental processing might hold for an understanding of voodoo and magical thinking. This is in preparation for the more generic examination of how symbolism, split-brain research, and bimodal mental processing relate to some phenomena of religion as we know it today.

Part Two

Split-Brain Research
and
Religious Experience

6

Religion, Bimodal Mental Processing, and the Unconscious

Humankind, in its quest for meaning, has developed the two great fields of religion and science, each sharing the distinction of being one of the great collective efforts in the human search for understanding. Each reflects the individual's quest for a feeling of solidarity and a sense of certainty. It is the product of this quest—the individual's belief system and world view— that sustains him in his struggles with the environment, with others, and with his own internal conflicts.

Both religion and science are the product of generations of thought and experience, and both reflect, to a greater or lesser degree, the human rational and intuitive genius. However, psychology, science's representative in the area of subjective experience, has not adequately established its relationship with religion, and the two are so intertwined with one another that it takes great effort to differentiate the two. In an attempt to clarify this situation, I will examine how certain aspects

123

of religious experience might be understood in terms of bimodal mental processing and the symbolic process.

THE EVOLUTION OF RELIGIOUS THOUGHT

In 1925, well before the split-brain experiments, Cassirer argued for the importance of symbolizing and for there being other "symbolic forms" besides language, and other modes of understanding besides reason per se. Of significance to our discussion here is Cassirer's observation of a similarity in the development and evolution of language and religion. While his ideas pertain to organized religion and take us away from the psychology of the individual, this examination of the evolution of religious thought is pertinent to our discussion, for it reflects the evolution of religious beliefs as human thought became less gestalt and more linear in nature.

Cassirer maintained that in the first stage of the development of language there was no distinction between the spoken word and its meaning—that which we have called adifferentiation, which is characteristic of the primacy of the gestalt mode of processing. There was in that early time an experiential unity between the word and its meaning; it was only gradually, over time, that there was an increasing differentiation between the "sign and the content," between the "sound and the significance," between the word and that for which it stood.

In its first beginnings the word still belongs to the sphere of mere existence: what is apprehended in it is not signification but rather a substantial being and power of its own. It does not point to an objective content but sets itself in the place of this content. . . . And what is true of the linguistic sign is true in the same sense of the written sign. The written word is not at once "apprehended" as such but is viewed as a part of the objective world, . . . as an extract of all the forces that are contained in it. All writing . . . replaces and "stands for" the object. . . . It is a magical instrument by which to gain possession of certain things and ward off hostile powers. . . . Long before the written sign is understood as an expression of an object it is feared as the substantial embodiment . . . of the forces that emanate from it, as a kind of demonic double of the object. Only when the magical feeling pales does man's attention turn from the empirical to the idea. (Cassirer 1955, pp. 237–238)

Cassirer made the intriguing point that the same evolution that occurred in language also occurred in human religious thinking. That is, whereas originally the mental images of supernatural significance were accepted as part of the "real" world of "things," gradually a differentiation was made.

We see the same relationship in the image world of myth (where the supernatural image) is so deeply embedded in man's intuition of the world of things . . . as to appear an integral part of it. Here again there is originally no division between the real and the ideal, between the sphere of "existence" and that of "meaning," but there is rather a continuous flux between the two spheres, both in man's thought and belief and in his action. . . . The dancer who appears in the mask of the god or demon does not merely imitate the god or demon but assumes his nature; he is transformed into him and fuses with him. Here there is never a mere image, an empty representation; nothing is thought, represented, "supposed" that is not at the same time real and effective. But in the gradual progress of the mythical world view a separation now begins, and it is this separation that constitutes the actual beginning of the specifically religious consciousness. The further back we follow it toward its origins, the less the content of religious consciousness can be distinguished from that of mythical consciousness. . . . If we attempt to isolate and remove the basic mythical components from religious belief, we no longer have religion in its real, objectively historical manifestation. (In the next stage) religion takes the decisive step that is essentially alien to myth: in its use of sensuous images and signs it recognizes them as such—a means of expression which, though they reveal a determinate meaning, must necessarily remain inadequate to it, which "point" to this meaning but never wholly exhaust it. (Cassirer 1955, pp. 238–239)

Cassirer goes on to say that, in its development, every great religion goes through this crisis of recognizing a symbol "as only" a symbol; as it does it breaks loose from what we have called adifferentiation. He suggests that perhaps the best example of this is in the Old Testament when Isaiah commanded that man shall not make false idols to worship and denounced the folly of man worshiping his own creations as something holy. Cassirer maintained that here we have religious intuition beholding the difference between the symbol and the thing for which it stands, an act fundamentally incompatible with what the anthropologists call "mythical thinking" where (in the language developed here) the gestalt mode predominates in one's thinking. It is at this point that religion emerges and becomes distinct from magic and superstition, for the polytheistic, pagan world view that the prophets were combating was not one in which there was mere worshiping of idols. In the pagan world view the believer held immediate possession of the deity, for with the predominance of the gestalt mode in his thinking, the pagan experienced a relative inability to separate himself from his world and his gods.

This question of seeing the difference between the symbol and that for which it stands is just the kind of controversy that surrounds the question of transubstantiation. And does the cross itself only "stand for" Christ or does it elicit the experience of the holy? The debate as to whether these images are to be taken literally or metaphorically is a debate that must be left to the clergy. But concerning this differentiation of the symbol from that for which it stands, Cassirer went on to talk specifically about what it means for Christianity per se.

In its whole development Christianity also fights this battle for its own peculiar definition of religious "reality." Here release from the world of mythical images seems all the more difficult because certain mythical intuitions are so deeply embedded in the fundamental doctrines, the dogmatic substance of Christianity, that they cannot be removed without endangering this substance itself. . . . Today . . . it can be said that there is scarcely a single feature in the world of Christian faith and ideas, scarcely a symbol, for which mythical-pagan parallels might not be shown. The entire history of dogmas, from the earliest beginnings down to Luther and Zwingli, indicates a constant struggle between the original historical significance of symbols, sacraments, and mysteries and their derived, purely spiritual meaning. (Cassirer 1955, pp. 247–248)

Cassirer gave a second example of a religion going through this crisis of recognizing the symbol "as only" a symbol. He pointed out that, according to Herodotus, the Persians also did not erect idols and temples to their god, for they, too, recognized that it was folly to do so. Like the God of the Prophets, Ahura Mazda, the Persian creator god, had no characteristics except that of "pure being and ethical goodness." Cassirer cited yet a third account of a great religion passing through this same crisis, but in a somewhat different fashion.

A third great example of how, in the progress of religious thought and speculation, the mythical world gradually sinks into nothingness and how this process spreads from the figures of myth to those of empirical existence may be found in the doctrine of the Upanishads. It . . . achieves its highest aim through negation. . . . The only name, the only designation, remaining for the absolute is negation itself. That which is, the atman, is call "No, No," and above this "this it is not" there is nothing. It is a final step along this same road when Buddhism extends the negation from object to subject. In the Prophetic-monotheistic religion, as religious thought and feeling are freed from the sphere of mere things, the reciprocal relation between the I and God becomes purer and more energetic. Liberation from the image and its objectivity has no other aim than to place this relation in the sharpest relief. Here the negation ultimately finds a fixed limit: it leaves untouched the center of the religious relationship, the individual and his self-consciousness. As the objective world recedes, a new mode of formation comes more and more distinctly to the fore: the formation of will and action. But Buddhism passes beyond this last barrier; for Buddhism the form of the I becomes just as accidental and external as any mere material form. The "truth" of Buddhism strives to surpass not only the world of things but the world of will and action as well. For it is precisely action and will that confine man to the cycle of becoming, that chain him to the "wheel of births." . . . Thus, true liberation lies not only beyond the world of things but above all beyond action and desire. . . . For (the Buddhist) the personality is no longer the kernel but the husk. . . . It possesses no permanence, no substantiality of its own. (Cassirer 1955, pp. 245–246)

A final point needs to be registered. It might be concluded from the previous discussion of Cassirer that modern, organized religion has moved away from what we have called adifferentiation, the inability to tell the difference between the symbol and that for which it stands. We suggest, however, that while organized religion has evolved in that direction, it has not left it entirely. Indeed, adifferentiation is very much involved in what religious scholars have called the *sine qua non* of religion, in that which has characterized religious experience throughout the ages.

THE *SINE QUA NON* OF RELIGION

Earlier I examined how language influences beliefs when I said that the language of the Trobriand Islanders is more gestalt in nature than our own. And I speculated how this gestalt quality in a language influences the individual toward a belief system that is full of magical powers and supernatural entities, and where reason attributes "cause" to these supernatural beings rather than to logically related, natural events.

Now as we follow what Cassirer had to say about the twin evolution of language and religious beliefs, we find confirming evidence of the importance of language in beliefs.

Cassirer suggested that religious beliefs changed over time, and what I have said about bimodal mental processing suggests that this change occurred as language and thought became progessively less gestalt-like and more linear in nature. In the process, the religious leaders were able to make distinctions between the symbol and the feeling for which it stood, something possible only when the linear mode increased in influence.

Let us turn now to another point: the significance that bimodal mental processing has for *personal* religious experience. One of the difficulties in such a discussion is that of finding a characteristic of religion that applies in all of its varied interpretations. But to speak of religion in any generic way one needs to identify some *sine qua non,* some thread that runs through all of what we call religion. James met with this same problem when in 1902 he wrote his classic *Varieties of Religious Experience.* His approach is so useful and so elegantly stated that I can do no better than to quote him as a statement of the position I shall take in the next few pages.

The field of religion being as wide (as it is) it would indeed be foolish to set up an arbitrary definition of religion's essence, and then proceed to defend that definition against all comers, yet this need not prevent me from taking my own narrow view of what religion shall consist in for the purpose of (this work) or, out of the many meanings of the word, from choosing the one meaning in which I wish to interest you particularly, and proclaiming arbitrarily that when I say "religion" I mean that. . . .

One way to mark it out easily is to say what aspects of the subject we leave out. At the outset we are struck by one great partition which divides the religious field. On the one side of it lies institutional, on the other personal religion. . . . Worship and sacrifice, procedures for working on the dispositions of the deity, theology and ceremony and ecclesiastical organization, are the essentials of religion in the institutional branch. Were we to limit our view to it, we should have to define religion as an external art, the art of winning the favor of the gods. In the more personal branch of religion it is on the contrary the inner disposition of man himself which forms the center of interest, his conscience, his deserts, his helplessness, his incompleteness. And although the favor of the God, as forfeited or gained, is still an essential feature of the story, and theology plays a vital part therein, yet the acts to which this sort of religion prompts are personal not ritual acts, the individual transacts the business by himself alone, and the ecclesiastical organization, with its priests and sacraments and other go-betweens, sinks to an altogether secondary place. The relation goes directly from heart to heart, from soul to soul, between man and his maker.

Now (at this point) I propose to ignore the institutional branch entirely, to say nothing of the ecclesiastical organizational branch entirely, to consider as little as possible the systematic theology and the ideas about the gods themselves, and to confine myself as far as I can to personal religion pure and simple. . . .

In one sense at least the personal religion will prove itself more fundamental than either theology or ecclesiasticism. Churches, when once established, live at second-hand upon tradition; but the *founders* of every church owed their power originally to the fact of their direct personal communion with the divine. Not only the superhuman founders, the Christ, the Buddha, Mohammed, but all the originators of Christian sects have been in this case;—so personal religion should still seem the primordial thing, even to those who continue to esteem it incomplete. (James 1903, pp. 35–37)

With this as a statement of how I shall be defining "religion," let me try to identify some *sine qua non,* some thread that runs through all of what we call religion. Although it might be hard to identify today in our (profane) world of "natural" events, we do in fact have just this type of thread, *the experience of "the holy" or "the sacred."* Certainly this is the case if we limit ourselves, like James, to personal religion.

THE SACRED, THE PROFANE, AND BIMODAL MENTAL PROCESSING

In 1917, Otto published *Das Heilige* (*The Sacred*), which has been acclaimed even to this day for its description of the frightening experience of feeling the presence of "the sacred" or "the holy." In this situation one experiences something totally different from that of the reality reflected through the senses, for one "knows" or experiences one's self to be in the presence of something "supernatural." The experience is characterized by Otto as (a) terrifying to an extreme degree and (b) giving the individual the impression that he is in the presence of something wholly separate from himself, called by Otto the "wholly other." For people living in the modern world of "natural" events, this process of "knowing" the reality of something unseen and supernatural is difficult to grasp. However, the accounts in the previous chapters on the beliefs of primitives can give an appreciation of this phenomenon. From an examination of this literature it is clear that for those experiencing the "wholly other," the unseen and "supernatural" world is as real as the experience of the reality of the "natural" world, and yet it is totally different.

Otto described the feeling of trembling, awe, mystery, and

fascination when feeling one's self to be in the presence of "the Divine," and he interpreted this experience as being *induced* by a divine power (more precisely, the experience is induced by the revelation of divine power). Otto maintained that this experience is at the very heart of religion and has been its essence throughout history. This is true not only for religion as we know it today but also during its evolutionary stages.

> It must be admitted that when religious evolution first begins sundry curious phenomena confront us, preliminary to religion proper and deeply affecting its subsequent course. Such are the notions "clean" and "unclean," belief in or worship of the dead, belief in or worship of "souls" or "spirits," magic, fairy tales, myths, homage to natural objects, whether frightful or extraordinary, noxious or advantageous, the strange idea of "power" (*Orenda* or *Manali*), fetishism and totemism, worship of animals and plants and demonism and polydemonism. Different as these things are, they are all haunted by a common (element) which is easily identifiable. (Otto 1982, p. 116)

The common element is of course the terrifying and awful experience of the "wholly other," "the sacred." Moreover, this experiencing of an unseen power (or witch or god) as wholly separate and distinct from one's self is, Otto maintained, evidence of the "actual existence" of an unseen "holy" presence, the Divine. Just as one's feeling of beauty arises in part as a reflection of the actual existence of something beautiful, this feeling of the presence of a Divine power is for Otto a reflection of the "actual existence" of an unseen but Divine reality. Such an interpretation is of course open to question, for the phenomenon could just as easily be seen as an experiential phenomenon of the believer himself, as an aspect of the "state of believing," needing no other reference point as such. In this case the emphasis would be placed upon the act of believing in the same way that, in the previous chapter, one might understand the native's "belief" in the reality of witches not to be supportive of the existence of the witches per se, but due to the inability of the primitive to distinguish between "objects" and ideas, "things" and images, so that an idea or image is experienced as real and as an object.

Otto himself recognized this, in a sense. In fact, he argued that the belief in the actual existence of demons and witches was a result of experiencing "the demonic." It was, he maintained, a "rationalization" of the feelings of awe and dread related to experiencing the "wholly other." However, he failed to use the same logic to conclude that the modern belief in God is likewise a "rationalization," perhaps of love, concern, and affection for those whose deity is a loving God. Instead, for Otto the experience of feeling one's self to be in the presence of the "Supreme and Sublime Deity" was evidence of the actual existence of the Divine and was no mere "rationalization," no mere mental phenomenon due to the nature of a particular mode of believing. Furthermore, individuals capable of such experiences, as was true of Otto himself, possessed the faculty of "divination."

It is precisely at this point where religion diverges from psychology as a science. This is important if one is to understand "believing" (including religious "believing"), in terms of the human being instead of Something or Someone "out there," instead of something "wholly other." Such an approach must conclude that one's belief in God is in fact a rationalization, an objectification of those feelings one attributes to God. This is the kind of language psychology must use, and the individual is the kind of reference point upon which a psychology must be based. However, it would seem to us a bit reductionistic to leave it at that, for *a psychology must be open to new and different possibilities, even the possibility that there is more to "God" than merely the rationalization of feelings.*

Psychology itself cannot disprove that there is Something or Someone "out there," but as a branch of science it must assume a different perspective. While religion finds it in the nature of the "supernatural" experience itself that one need look no further for understanding, psychology must focus on the experience of the individual and place this phenomenon into a context of understanding that does not assume supernatural realities. Moreover, even if religion's assertions are assumed to be true, it will only gain from psychology's efforts, for the comfort and reassurance that religion has to offer will only be enhanced by its integration with a broader and more flexible understanding.

Be that as it may, one cannot minimize the importance of Otto and his description of the individual's experience of "the sacred," for it is clear that this experience has been of utmost importance throughout the history of religion. For religious scholars this comes as no revelation; but for most of us who have lived a "profane" life and have not been familiar with the experience of "the sacred," the identification of this experience as the *sine qua non* of religion offers a new insight and a new way of understanding at least some aspects of religious phenomena. For instance, another religious scholar, Eliade, in his book *The Sacred and the Profane,* echoed the same point made by Otto.

It could be said that the history of religion—from the most primitive to the most highly developed—is constituted by a great number . . . of . . . manifestations of the sacred in some ordinary object, a stone or a tree—to the supreme (which for a Christian, is the incarnation of God in Jesus Christ) there is no dissolution of continuity. In each case we are confronted by the same mysterious act—the manifestation of something of a wholly different order, a reality that does not belong to our world, in objects that are an integral part of our natural "profane world."

The modern Occidental experiences a certain uneasiness before many manifestations of the sacred. He finds it difficult to accept the fact that, for many human beings, the sacred can be manifested in stones or trees, for example. But . . . what is involved is not a veneration of the stone in itself, a cult of the tree in itself. The sacred tree, the sacred stone are not adored as stone or tree; they are worshipped precisely because they . . . show something that is no longer stone or tree but sacred, the ("wholly other"). (Eliade 1959, pp. 11–12)

Eliade then goes on to elaborate on the idea that throughout the ages the hallmark of religion has been this phenomenon of experiencing something "wholly other" as an unseen reality, the experience of the sacred or Divine as manifesting itself in the natural world. Whereas modern individuals consider such acts as eating, having sex, hunting, crossing a stream, planting corn, etc., as only behavioral acts, for the primitive these acts became "a sacrament . . . a communion with the sacred" (Eliade 1959, p. 14). The primitive lived in a "sacralized cosmos." According to this view, the essential difference between the mind of modern man and that of the primitive is this existential mode of being in the world. Thus "the sacred" and "the profane" become two modes of "being in the world," two modes of believing and viewing reality. And the same mode of "being in" and viewing the world that was true of the primitive can be seen as characterizing religious experience throughout the course of history.

This point, which Otto and Eliade make, is pivotal in examining the relationship between bimodal mental processing and at least some aspects of religion; so let us look at it more closely. First Otto and Eliade *observe,* from examining written and oral accounts, that the history of religion is the history of experiencing the *feeling* of being in the presence of sacred, unseen realities or entities. Second, they assume the existence of the latter.

The radically different approach of psychology can agree with their *observation* but not endorse their assumption. From a psychological perspective, the observed phenomenon can be seen as an expression, not of some *assumed* deity but of the individual's state of believing. A feeling is symbolized by an image, as a feeling of fear is symbolized by the image of a witch, and in this mode of believing no distinction is made between the image and external reality. We have termed the inability to separate the symbol from that for which it stands as "adifferentiation," and we have used the term "objectification" for the experience of feeling a mental image to be in the "outside," objective world.

I suggest that because of adifferentiation and objectification the symbolized feelings are experienced not as mental phenomena but as objects in the objective world. Conceptualizing this as a psychological process rather than as evidence of a supernatural entity turns us toward the individual and away from speculations about unseen realities. It allows us to examine some aspects or phenomena of personal religion, not in terms of supernatural entities but as products of a particular mode of believing, and in terms of reasoned concepts acceptable to psychology and science in general.

In spite of the fact that a modern psychological perspective might interpret Otto differently, his work remains a landmark in the examination of religious experience. He considered himself to be working within the psychology of religion, and in this capacity he was unique for his time. Working at a time when psychology was beginning to look more carefully at the phenomenon of the human religious experience, Otto's work was important in that his was the first to look carefully at the different parameters of experiencing "the sacred" and to identify clearly the "wholly other." As such his work is important, for it allows us to identify what has been the hallmark of personal religious experience throughout the ages. If we focus on his observations and descriptions instead of his conclusions, we become aware that *a predominance of the gestalt mode of processing and the experiences of adifferentiation and objectification has been characteristic of personal religious experience throughout history, resulting in the* sine qua non *of religion, the feeling of being in the presence of unseen powers and entities, the experience of feeling the reality of the "wholly other."*

From examining Otto's remarks, it seems evident that the previous examples of primitive beliefs in voodoo, witches, the evil eye, and magic fall well within what he called "the sacred." If one accepts, as I have attempted to demonstrate, that one of the factors in these beliefs is the predominance of the "gestalt" mode of processing, then it is understandable when the religious individual says that one cannot understand through "reason" alone, for it entails a mode of believing in which discursive reason and the linear mode of processing recede into the background. It suggests an understanding of

the occasion when at Holy Communion some believers construe the bread and wine to be the body and blood of Christ.
It is more understandable that the enactment of a religious
ceremony brings a belief to life, not merely as a mimicking
of some past event, but as a supernatural "living" or "being
in" a sacred event. Furthermore, it is more understandable
that, for instance, one might feel a unity with God via a
symbol like a Star of David or a cross, for the predominance
of feeling" and the lack of separateness characteristic of gestalt
processing allows for the "feeling of unity" that is missing
with a predominance of the linear mode. More understandable
as well is the fact that at times reason is suspended in religious
experiencing and believing, and instead emotions dominate.
Finally, the religious concept of faith is understood to include
"a feeling of solidarity or firmness" in addition to a rational
set of statements.

An important point should be made here: I have not
addressed the question of whether "truth" is reflected by our
feelings as well as by reason. My hunch is that it is, but
this is too large a question to go into at this point. If in
fact truth is "felt," then the feeling of there being a Sacred
Being may reflect a truth regardless of whether it is "merely"
an objectification of one's own feelings. This is an important
question, but one we are not yet equipped to answer. If it
eventually proves to be true, it would argue for a Sacred
Being that is less concrete in nature and for a belief system
that is more flexible than some would presently possess.

I have suggested that bimodal mental processing offers
an approach to understanding at least some aspects of religious
experience. First, it lets us understand a particular crisis in
the evolution of every great religion: the point where it emerges
from a background of magic and superstition to become

religion per se. The inability to make distinctions, so characteristic of the gestalt mode, presents itself to the religious believer as an inability to distinguish a symbol from that for which the symbol stands; an inability to distinguish an idol, for instance, from the purely religious feeling it represents. According to Cassirer, in the evolution of every great religion there is a crisis point where this inability is overcome, and the religious leaders are able to break away from a world view dominated by magic and superstition. In terms of the ideas presented here, they are able to break away from a way of thinking (and thus believing) that is completely dominated by the gestalt mode of processing. They emerge from a world where cause and effect are determined by wishes and feelings, where there is a lack of distinction between events and individuals, and where time and space do not restrain one's sense of reality.

Second, an insight into bimodal mental processing helps us understand the experience of "the sacred," that personal religious experience that Otto and Eliade suggest is the *sine qua non* of religion at all levels. Here the modern Western world of logically related events and separate entities fades away, and time, cause, and identity become related via feelings and desires. And the individual's feelings are experienced as external, for they are felt to be supernatural and to have their own life and energy.

It seems we have seen a steady and progressive change in the form of religious experiencing paralleling the progressive decline in the influence of the gestalt mode. First came superstition and magical thinking, and then came the crises where religion per se emerged, as Cassirer said, from myth, as religious feelings became distinct from their symbols. Now, with the further decline in the influence of the gestalt mode, we see an apparent contradiction. If the experience of "the sacred" is indeed the *sine qua non* of religion, as Otto and Eliade suggest, and if the influence of this experience is generally on the decline, as Eliade suggests, then does this mean the impending end of religion or, to use Nietzsche's term, the death of God? If so, the decline of influence of the gestalt mode marks both the birth and the death of religion. Or is religion, which has survived so many scrimmages with science and so many advancements in thought, merely going through another temporary readjustment in order to regroup and reformulate itself in terms consistent with a more modern line of thought?

These are questions I cannot answer. At this point I will proceed with my own project of formulating a concept of religion from a psychological perspective that may be acceptable to skeptics who insist on reason and logic rather than mystery in their beliefs. That is, I will explore how our formulations about "the sacred" relate to the *unconscious,* a term that is more consistent with science and psychology than with traditional religion.

PERSONAL RELIGIOUS EXPERIENCE AND THE UNCONSCIOUS

In the Introduction I suggested that psychology, as it now stands, is incomplete because it has not found a satisfactory way of including within its purview those very attributes that make us most human: emotion, value, willing, believing, etc. Psychotherapy—psychology's chief representative in the arena of practical application—does indeed deal on a daily basis with such issues, but for the most part it has been treated as a stepchild by science in general: tolerated but not respected. To be truthful, there is some justification for this attitude, for psychotherapy has yet to find a useful way of incorporating these subjectively human issues into a scheme of thought that is scientifically credible. The movement of humanistic psychology was, in a sense, conceived and born as a response to widespread doubts about the validity of the then prevalent psychological theories that were weak in the areas of value, intension, and feeling. The formulations of the scholars and therapists within this movement were eloquent and insightful, and they certainly humanized psychology's concepts, but they never were successful in developing their interests into a form that could be included within the body of science. Religion, humankind's other great effort to account for subjective experience, has not been so remiss, for such issues as valuing and believing lie at the heart of its formulations. However, its supernatural assumptions are at odds with scientific scrutiny, and from an objective viewpoint we are faced with the prospect of discarding these issues altogether or accepting them as encrusted within the supernatural.

I maintain, however, that there is a third option, that of formulating such issues as believing, valuing, willing, feeling, etc., in terms that are consistent with science and objective observations. I maintain that psychology (and psychotherapy) and religion are essentially dealing with the same area when they direct their interests to human subjective experience, but they are using different languages. It is the proverbial story of the blind men looking at the same elephant, each describing it in different ways, except that in this case they use different languages, languages based on different and incompatible assumptions. One of these blind men talks of neurons and brain function or uses such terms as "the self," while the second speaks of the "soul." One speaks of altered states of consciousness; the other talks of miracles and personal religious experience. My purpose here is to make an initial attempt to suggest the beginnings of a conceivable framework for understanding psychology (and psychotherapy), neurology, and at least some aspects of religion, a framework that might include the unconscious, religious experience, and split-brain research within the same understanding.

In 1902, James concluded his epic work on *The Varieties of Religious Experience* with a plea for the establishment of a science of religions. He argued eloquently that religion must be taken seriously; and after reviewing the varieties of religious experience he asked the question ". . . is there, under all the discrepancies of the creeds, (of the various religions) a common nucleus to which they bear their testimony unanimously?" (James 1903, p. 509). His answer to this question was unequivocally yes. "The warring Gods and formulas of the various religions do indeed cancel each other, but there is a certain uniform deliverance in which religions all appear to meet" (James 1903, pp. 507–508). He characterized this deliverance as a feeling that:

> . . . we are saved from . . . a sense of uneasiness that something is wrong with us . . . by making proper connection with the higher powers . . . (and becoming conscious that a) . . . higher part (of ourselves) is coterminous and continuous with more of the same quality. . . . (James 1903, p. 509)

After examining numerous varieties of the religious experience of becoming conscious of a "connection with the higher powers," James went on to say:

. . . The experiences are only psychological phenomena. They possess, it is true, enormous biological worth. Spiritual strength really increases in the subject when he has them, a new life opens for him, and they seem to him a place of conflux where the forces of two universes meet; and yet this may be nothing but his subjective way of feeling things, a mood of his own fancy, in spite of the effects produced. (James 1903, p. 509)

James went on to point out that the feeling of being in contact with "a more of the same quality" within the world itself is a key point. Our "higher part" comes into a harmonious working relationship with this "more of the same quality," and it is in trying to establish the nature of this "more" that the various religions differ in their view.

It is in answering these questions that the various theologies perform their theoretic work, and that their divergencies most come to light. They all agree that the "more" really exists; though some of them hold it to exist in the shape of a personal god or gods, while others are satisfied to conceive it as a stream of ideal tendency embedded in the eternal structure of the world. They all agree, moreover, that it acts as well as exists, and that something really is effected for the better when you throw your life into its hands. It is when they treat of the experience of "union" with it that their speculative differences appear most clearly. Over this point pantheism and theism, nature and second birth, works and grace and karma, immortality and reincarnation, rationalism and mysticism, carry on their inveterate disputes. (James 1903, p. 509)

. . . Here mysticism and the conversion-rapture and Vedantism and transcendental idealism bring in their monastic interpretations and tell us that the finite self rejoins the absolute self. . . . Here the prophets of all the different religions come with their visions, voices, raptures, and other openings, supposed by each to authenticate his own peculiar faith. (James 1903, p. 513–514)

James next wondered if, out of the various religions with respect to the nature of this "more" and the possible "connection" with it, we "might sift out from the discrepancies a common body of doctrine which (we might) formulate in terms to which physical science need not object."

It would never do for us to place ourselves offhand at the position of a particular theology, the Christian theology, for example, and proceed immediately to define the "more" as Jehovah, and the "union" as his imputation to us of the righteousness of Christ. That would be unfair to other religions. . . . (James 1903, p. 510)

We must begin by using less particularized terms; and, since one of the duties of the science of religions is to keep religion in connection with the rest of science, we shall do well to seek first of all a way of describing the "more" which psychologists may also recognize as real. The *subconscious self* is nowadays a well-accredited psychological entity; and I believe that in it we have exactly the mediating term required. . . .

Let me then propose . . . that . . . the "more" with which in religious experience we feel ourselves connected is on its *hither* side the subconscious continuation of our conscious life. Starting thus with a recognized psychological fact as our basis, we seem to preserve a contact with "science" which the ordinary theologian lacks. At the same time the theologian's contention that the religious man is moved by an external power is vindicated, for it is one of the peculiarities of invasions from the subconscious region to take on objective appearances, and to suggest to the Subject an external control. In the religious life the control is felt as "higher"; but (in) our hypothesis it is primarily the higher faculties of our own hidden mind which are controlling. . . . (James 1903, pp. 512–513)

With his observation made in 1902 that "invasions from the subconscious . . . take on objective appearances (suggesting) an external control," James has given us a truly ingenious observation that has been ignored by generations of psychologists and psychiatrists. James reviewed an extraordinary number of reports of individuals who had had a personal religious experience, and he basically agreed with Otto (or vice versa, since he wrote some years before Otto) that all the reported accounts were essentially examples and variations of *one* fundamental experience. Otto called this basic experience the "sacred" and, being a churchman, he conceived of it as evidence of the presence and existence of God. While not discounting Otto's point, and even acknowledging his own personal preference for it, James, writing as a psychologist, viewed this basic experience as "purely" an individual psychological experience. And even though James and Otto used different languages and labored under different sets of assumptions, on reading their accounts, one reaches the conclusion that the psychologist and the churchman were describing the same phenomenon. That is, James gave a psychological accounting for what Otto later would call the *sine qua non* of religion, the experience of "the sacred."

We can at this point tie together two different ideas: (1) James's view that the various interpretations of religious experience reflect "invasions from the subconscious" that are felt as an external control, and (2) the observation by Otto that the hallmark of religion throughout the ages has been the experience of "the sacred," which is characteristically described as an unseen, terrifying presence of something "wholly other" and separate from one's self. Considered together, these two ideas warrant the conclusion that *the hallmark of religion throughout the ages has been an experience that can be understood as "invasions" from the unconscious that are felt as separate and "wholly other" from one's self.* This formulation may meet with much resistance from those who would rather not formulate the fundamental criteria of religious experience in psychological terms, but they need not be concerned for religion's sake. As has been suggested, religion has much to gain from a careful analysis of human psychology.

BIMODAL MENTAL PROCESSING AND THE UNCONSCIOUS

How can bimodal mental processing relate to the experience of "the sacred" and "the wholly other" as described by Otto? Or, to put it in James's words, how do "invasions from the subconscious" relate to bimodal mental processing? These are extremely important but very difficult questions. However, if psychology is ever to extend its theory into the experiential, it must give an answer. It must attempt to include "invasions from the subconscious," "the sacred," the "wholly other," and bimodal mental processing within one framework of understanding, within a unity of thought.

In dealing with these issues I shall develop a new formulation of the unconscious. It will be consistent with some of Freud's *observations* about unconscious processes, yet it is less metaphysical and more clearly grounded in experimental research than is classical (or even modern) psychoanalytic theory. While the ideas to be set forth do not represent a complete psychological formulation of the unconscious (because we want to remain generally within the bounds of our present thesis about psychology and religious experience), they do offer a fresh approach, one that is significant for psychology generally and for psychotherapy in particular. But the unconscious cannot be addressed without understanding "consciousness"; thus, the task ahead will be to examine what I prefer to call "conscious awareness."

7

Conscious Awareness and "Invasions" from the Unconscious

CONSCIOUS AWARENESS

I introduced in chapter 6 the idea, that from a psychological perspective, the unconscious is important to an understanding of religious phenomena. The time has come to look at "consciousness," an understanding of which acts as a backdrop for any discussion of the unconscious. I shall begin by suggesting a different terminology, for the term "consciousness" is too broad and has too many established connotations. To reduce confusion, I intend to concentrate instead on the term "awareness," for this would allow for the possibility of other types of awareness besides that which we ordinarily call "consciousness." I shall therefore use *conscious awareness* to indicate what is ordinarily experienced as consciousness. This refers to our normal state of awareness in our waking life and does not apply to the awareness experienced during

149

"altered states of consciousness," as in daydreams, what are termed hypnotic "trances," or in any of "the varieties of religious experience." I suggest here, in anticipation of further elaboration later, that in these "altered states" awareness is dominated and determined by feelings rather than sensory impressions and rational understanding.

CONSCIOUSLY AWARE OF WHAT?

In using the term "conscious awareness," we must still ask ourselves what is it that we are consciously aware of? And how does human conscious awareness differ from that of our animal cousins? First, we are aware of things we see and hear, sensory images that reflect our experience of the outside world. Second, we are aware of sensations, such as the feeling of pain from a distended bladder or an intestinal cramp. And third, we are aware of emotions, such as the thrill of a ride on a roller coaster or the fear of impending danger. This awareness of sensory images, sensations, and emotions is, it would seem, shared by our animal cousins. Can we not, for instance, assume that they are aware of the momentary images and sensations that seem to flow from their sensory organs, and although it might be debated, can we not also assume that they are aware of such emotions as fear and anger?

Likewise, can we not assume that conscious awareness for human beings includes more than what the cow or the ape can experience? From the previous discussion about the symbolic process, we can say that it is the use of symbols that sets human mentation and conscious awareness apart from that of the animals. Thus at this time a distinction can be drawn between an *unsymbolized awareness*—such as the simple awareness of sensory images, sensations, or emotions— and a *symbolized awareness*—such as an awareness of language or of the symbolic meaning of a skull and crossbones. Conscious awareness for animals would include the former but not the latter. That is, we can assume that they are aware of sensations as well as sensory images and emotions, but they are not capable of using the former to symbolize the latter. For animals, conscious awareness seems to be simply an unsymbolized awareness of sensations, sensory images, perceptions, and emotions. Humans, however, are capable of symbolized as well as unsymbolized awareness. They are capable of combining sensory forms and emotions into a symbol, an act that is basically beyond the abilities of other animals. Humans are therefore capable of using sensory forms to symbolize the unsensed portion of themselves.

Having established that to understand the unconscious (unconscious awareness) requires a prior understanding of conscious awareness, and that in humans the latter includes a symbolic awareness, let us consider more precisely what conscious awareness is for the human being. Specifically, I suggest it is *both an unsymbolized awareness and a symbolized awareness:* an unsymbolized awareness of sensations, emotions, and sensory images plus a symbolized awareness of meanings structured by a system of natural language. This last point about natural language introduces a new parameter, so at this point let us go on to examine some of the split-brain research that supports the importance of language in this formulation.

Language and Conscious Awareness

At first it jars the understanding to suggest that conscious awareness is related to language. It is like saying apple pie is made from oranges, so foreign does language appear in relation to conscious awareness. Specifically, I suggest and attempt to offer a rationale for understanding that *conscious awareness is, among other things, an awareness of symbolic meanings structured by our natural language system.*

I shall try at this point to "ground" these ideas on experimental research so as not to be accused of metaphysical speculations. I refer the reader to chapter 2 in which experimental evidence was derived from the split-brain patients. It clearly suggests an unusual and special relationship between "awareness" and our language system.

A series of experiments led Gazzaniga and LeDoux to suggest that humans create "a personal sense of conscious reality" (1978, p. 150) built on their verbal or natural language system. My position is slightly different: I feel that "consciousness" cannot be reduced to the status of a product of only our language system, for other parameters contribute as well; but it does seem that the structure provided by natural language contributes to a sense of stability in an individual's world view. In other words, I cannot at this point identify all of the factors contributing to consciousness, but there is good evidence to suggest that natural language (or whatever system on which it is based) does contribute stability to conscious awareness.

I shall provide a brief review of some of the experiments that led Gazzaniga and LeDoux to their conclusion, an important position that seems to have implications for understanding the unconscious. In chapter 2, I referred to a patient who had been asked to select from among a group of pictures the one that best related to a scene that had been flashed on a screen. For the sake of continuity, I shall again refer to this example. The experiment was done in such a manner that a snow scene was presented to the right hemisphere and a chicken claw was presented to the left, and the subject pointed with the associated hand to a snow shovel and a chicken. When asked why he made those particular selections, he responded, "I saw a claw and I picked the chicken, and you have to clean out the chicken shed with a shovel" (Gazzaniga & LeDoux 1978, p. 148). This is a clear example of the left hemisphere, where language is for the most part processed, fabricating for its own purposes an "explanation" of the action of the right hemisphere. (It is interesting that in this case the right hemisphere seemed "logical" in its selection of a snow shovel to match the snow scene, but it seemed unable to express that logic in words.)

> In trial after trial, we saw this kind of response. The left hemisphere could easily and accurately identify why it had picked the answer, and then subsequently, and without batting an eye, it would incorporate the right hemisphere's response into the framework. While we knew exactly why the right hemisphere had made its choice, the left hemisphere could merely guess. Yet, the left did not offer its suggestion in a guessing vein but rather as a statement of fact as to why that card had been picked. (Gazzaniga & LeDoux 1978, pp. 148-149)

In one experiment a woman subject blushed and giggled. She seemed to fabricate a reason for her emotional response when in fact it was apparent to the experimenters that her embarrassment was generated by a picture of a nude being flashed to the right, nonverbal hemisphere (Sperry 1968). In this case it could be argued that, in some sense, her sympathetic nervous system was "aware" of the picture while at the same time her "awareness" did not include her verbal system. However, this is certainly not what we ordinarily think of as "consciousness."

Just as the left hemisphere was unaware of the "reason" for the behavior generated by the right hemisphere and would fabricate a "reason" for it, the same was true for emotional responses. When a subject, in this case an adolescent boy, was instructed via the right hemisphere to kiss someone:

> . . . the left blurted out, "Hey, no way, no way. You've got to be kidding." When asked what it was that he was not going to do, he was unable to tell us. Later, we presented "kiss" to the left hemisphere and a similar response occurred: "Hey, no way, I'm not going to kiss you guys." However, this time the speaking half-brain knew what the word was. In both instances, the command "kiss" elicited an emotional reaction that was detected by the verbal system of the left hemisphere, and the overt verbal response of the left hemisphere was basically the same, regardless of whether the command was presented to the right or left half-brain. In other words, the verbal system of the left hemisphere seemed to be able to accurately read the emotional tone and direction of a word seen by the right hemisphere alone. (Gazzaniga & LeDoux 1978, p. 151)

Due in large part to split-brain experiments, the question of the relationship of conscious awareness to the neural system is now a matter of much speculation. It has been demonstrated that after cutting the corpus callosum in human subjects, "each surgically disconnected hemisphere appears to have a mind of its own, with each cut off from, and oblivious to . . . events in the partner hemisphere" (Sperry 1985, p. 15). Objects identified by either hand separately can later be identified and separated from other objects by the respective hand. Smells experienced through one nostril are not recognized through the other, and objects visually exposed to one hemisphere cannot be recognized by the other (Sperry 1985, p. 15). In other words, when input is carefully restricted to one hemisphere, there is no recognition by the other hemisphere either through verbal or motor response. In many instances there is good evidence for the perception and recognition of test objects by either hemisphere but no evidence exists that the two parts of the brain communicate with each other.

A controversy arises, however, regarding how this data is to be interpreted. Is conscious awareness restricted to the verbal hemisphere or to that hemisphere plus the brainstem? Is the nonspeaking hemisphere only "a computer-like, unconscious automaton"? Does each hemisphere have a "personal identity" of its own, in which case cutting the corpus callosum would only reveal a duality that already exists, a duality that normally goes undetected because of the functional synchronicity of the two hemispheres under normal conditions? On the other hand, is the nonverbal hemisphere just as "conscious" as its verbal counterpart, but simply mute? Is "the conscious mind . . . single and unified (involving) both hemispheres" (Sperry 1985, p. 21)?

An intermediate position between limiting conscious awareness to the verbal hemisphere or considering both hemispheres as equally "conscious," concedes that the hemisphere that lacks language nonetheless "possesses consciousness" at some level but not the "higher, reflective, and self-conscious awareness that characterizes the human mind and (that) is needed . . . to qualify a conscious system as a person" (Sperry 1985, pp. 19–20). Exactly what it would take to qualify as a "person" is left a bit hazy, although in this position self-awareness is considered an essentially human attribute and as such represents a relatively advanced phase of conscious awareness deserving of special consideration (Sperry 1985, p. 20). The evidence here is that the individual is capable of recognizing his own image through either hemisphere when, for instance, that image is presented in the form of his photograph or his reflection in a mirror (Sperry 1985, p. 22). If this self-awareness indicates conscious awareness, then this bilateral capacity to recognize one's self would argue for conscious awareness being an attribute of either hemisphere.

What makes human awareness unique is the ability to symbolize. What is called "self-conscious awareness" or self awareness is simply a reflection of the organism's ability to recognize the self symbolically. In experiments where a person is able to recognize his own photograph or his reflection in a mirror, we are witnessing the individual's ability to recognize the image as a symbol of the self. It is a symbol of those "fixed" elements that have been integrated into a "self," into a gestalt that we symbolically call the self.

Another way of considering the anatomical correlations to conscious awareness is expressed by Gazzaniga (1985), a view that is particularly interesting because it relates not only to the concept of consious awareness but also to the idea of the unconscious. He suggests that the human brain is organized into more or less independent modules, and that the mind does not solve problems in some single way but functions instead as independent systems that work parallel to one another on the same problem. The human brain takes the vast array of informational elements impinging on it and breaks them into groups that are handled by different systems or modules. Visual cues may be handled by a different module than tactile cues, and both are different from the module that handles language functions. These various modules can compute, remember, feel emotion, and act; they may or may not be in touch with the natural language system and those cognitive systems underlying conscious awareness.

Observing that ordinary conscious life finds us doing things or having thoughts that seem to come from nowhere, Gazzaniga suggests that such thoughts or actions originate from these modular systems. Furthermore, he speculates that there is a special brain component that he calls the "interpreter," which constructs a theory to explain the behaviors that occur, a theory represented in the human language system. A module might react to stimuli that trigger an emotional response, for instance, and this response can be communicated to the left-hemisphere's verbal system related to conscious awareness, while the latter remains unaware of the stimuli that triggered the response in the first place. This system, he suggests, is basically consistent with Freud's theory of the unconscious—if Freud's concept of "unconscious processes" is changed to the idea of "co-conscious but nonverbal mental modules" (Gazzaniga 1985, p. 117). These are provocative words, especially when written by one of the world's leading neuropsychologists.

The idea of parallel mental systems operating simultaneously is intriguing in its possible consistency with both anatomical factors and psychoanalytic thoughts about the unconscious, but working out the details of such correspondence needs considerable refinement from both the organic and the psychodynamic perspectives. However, how the anatomical questions are eventually worked out is not our concern here. I have already stressed that a sharp distinction must be made between anatomical and psychological (mental) matters. Current understanding of neurological systems does not provide enough information to answer all the crucial questions, but this should not keep us from looking at how experience as a whole is organized. It is only by carefully separating these concepts that we can hope eventually to unite them into an integrated understanding.

Thus, I leave to others the questions about neural organization and the "location" of conscious awareness. Instead, I shall concentrate on the psychological or experiential side of the equation. First, it is my contention that no matter how the anatomical questions are answered, it will still hold true that the human mind organizes experience in two basic ways: the linear and gestalt modes of mental processing. Second, the importance of the symbolic process must be appreciated by any legitimate approach that desires to understand conscious awareness and the unconscious. It is the integration of these two concepts (bimodal mental processing and the symbolic process) that attracts our attention here; that and the question of how they might bear on the concepts of conscious awareness and the unconscious.

CONSCIOUS AWARENESS AS AN UNSYMBOLIZED AWARENESS PLUS A STRUCTURED SYMBOLIC AWARENESS

I maintain that *conscious awareness arises from the integration of an unsymbolized awareness and a symbolized awareness, the latter being a meaning expressed in one's natural language system.* It is an awareness that is in part shared with our animal cousins and in part unique to humans, the latter being an awareness and understanding expressed in our natural language system. The uniquely human awareness provides a structure that is either loose or firm depending on whether the particular natural language is more gestalt or more linear in nature. The gestalt mode allows for beliefs in which feelings, emotions, desires, and the like strongly influence concepts of time, space, identity, and cause. This was noted when the beliefs of primitives were examined. However, when the linear mode is the dominant influence on language and thus thinking, it allows for time, cause, and identity to be defined more or less as they are in the modern, Western world.

As I write, I am aware of the whiteness of the tablet sheet and of a vague ache in my muscles from exercising the previous day. I am, in short, aware of sensory input that conveys no symbolic message. But I am also aware of the words I have written, the message they symbolize, and the thoughts they communicate. My awareness is both unsymbolized and symbolized; the latter makes me different from an ape or a cow.

Yet, as I sit at my desk composing these thoughts, I take for granted a world view (an understanding of the world) that is built from sensory perceptions and their conceived relationships, an understanding that for the most part remains outside of my conscious awareness. Just as one might flash a spotlight across a tapestry, briefly illuminating details that otherwise remain hidden, so I can briefly focus my attention on one or another portion of my world view. And while the focus of my conscious awareness may briefly illuminate only small areas at any one time, a consistency unites the various impressions into a whole. There in the background, providing a structure and consistency to my conscious awareness, is my world view, a matrix of images related in my perceptual fields and through an understanding conceived in thought.

For the ancient Egyptians this tapestry of understanding included the idea of a great, sacred sky beetle that rolled the ball of the sun across the sky each day. For the medieval European it included the belief in angels who kept the heavenly bodies in their proper places. For most of us today it includes the belief that the sun rises in the East and sets in the West; and for the modern physicist it includes assumptions about the Copernican theory, the relativity theory, and forces between the planets and stars that are proportional to the square of the distance between them. Understanding, then, structured and understood in a natural language system, is there to maintain the integrity and continuity of the backdrop upon which the human mind focuses its conscious awareness. (This idea of world view and its structural and feeling components is elaborated upon in Appendix II.)

WHERE HAVE WE GONE SO FAR?

I have referred to James and Otto and have suggested that the unconscious is important for an understanding of personal religious experience. Because the unconscious cannot be understood prior to acquiring an appreciation of "consciousness," I have discussed the nature of conscious awareness, concluding that human conscious awareness arises from the integration of an unsymbolized awareness of sensations, emotions, and sensory images with a symbolized awareness that is structured by a natural language system. However, this only advances the discussion part of the way, for I have yet to examine the unconscious and the "invasions" that emerge from it.

"INVASIONS" FROM THE UNCONSCIOUS

How does the individual navigate in the world of objects outside of the self? It would seem that the mind creates some type of "map" of the world. How can a person drive a car down the highway, for instance, without a set of mental images that correspond to the highway, the hood of the car, the onrushing traffic in the opposite lane, and so on? These images, then, help the individual navigate safely and successfully to intended destinations. Such imagery is necessary for every successful human action, from emptying the garbage to throwing a touchdown pass. I suggest, then, that the human mind creates a world view, essentially a "map" of the world. It is, to be sure, a special kind of map where specific images are analogous to objects in the world and perceived relationships between objects are analogously reflected in the map.

But doesn't a world view represent *more* than the outside world? Doesn't it also have meaning and represent personal feelings about the world—i.e., values, intentions, likes, and dislikes? Certainly. A world view, that which seemingly guides (or perhaps propels) the self in its dealings with the world, emerges as a result of the integration of subjective and objective experiences. It results from the integration of a sense of self and a sense of the world. But how are feelings and values incorporated into a map? How is meaning represented? The pivotal point in answering these questions rests with how the human mind "knows" itself and the world.

Knowing Self and World

How do we come to "know" the self and the world? Certainly one way is through the formation of sensory images, for our common sense suggests that we "know" a tree, for instance, when we see it. (See Appendix III for further discussion of this.) But if we "know" the world through our sensory imagery, the question naturally arises as to how we "know" that part of ourselves that does not have access to our sense organs, in other words, our emotions, feelings, values, intentions, and the like? The primary way is through the symbolic process: perceptual images can symbolize the "felt" portion of subjective experience. *That is, perceptual images can function in two ways.* They can represent elements in an analogue map and, as such, they can represent objects and relationships in the world. But they can also symbolize feelings, and, in so doing, perceptual images add *life* and feeling to the world view. Feelings are fleeting, growing and subsiding and changing from situation to situation and from time to time. When contrasted with the structured relationships of mathematics and perceptual fields, feelings, though fleeting, fluid, and impermanent, are nevertheless filled with *life* and symbolized by perceived images and forms.

Thus, because the elements of the map are images that can symbolize feelings, the mind's world view is something more than simply an analogue map, for it also reflects emotion, intention, significance, meaning, and value within subjective experience. In short it has *life.* Thus it is more that a simple analogue map that might represent the structured relationships of a territory or country with its rivers, mountains, cities, and counties. It would do that of course, but it would also have areas of the map at times being *alive* and *feeling,* as if this river or that mountain were fleetingly *alive with movement and emotion.*

A Problem

Because a mental image can function for a human being as either an element in the structure of the analogue map of a world view or as a symbolic expression of subjective feelings, a problem arises for humans that does not present itself to other animals. What happens when attention is focused on a particular element of this "map" or world view? Is awareness primarily concentrated on the "feeling" connotations of that particular element or does the structural background take center stage? Gestalt psychologists have taught that when observing a particular figure or image the observer is not simply aware of an isolated image. Instead, the observer is aware of the figure as it is situated within a field or context. Philosophers have argued that the contextual notion of "meaning" suggests that an item "means" something according to the context within which it is embedded. (A triangle within an oval "means" a nose.) Taken together these ideas suggest that when an element or image is perceived it is experienced within a context that determines its meaning, a meaning that is reasoned and structured or based upon feeling and emotional, depending on whether structure or feelings dominate the background.

When we look at mathematical equations, we are aware of the related elements. We are aware, for example, that two plus two equals four. With mathematics we are in the arena of pure abstraction, for two plus two could be two fish or two trees or two anything. We are removed from sensory imagery and thus removed from any emotional connotations they might carry. Our conscious awareness is restricted to structure alone.

When attention is focused on a particular stock on the

exchange, it is seen within the framework of what one knows about that particular company, the industry to which it belongs, and general market conditions. It is seen within the structure of the available information and one's linguistically formulated understanding of the situation in which that particular stock is embedded.

When looking at a familiar photograph, the viewer becomes vaguely aware of nostalgic feelings that are connotations of the image itself. Similarly, when a deeply religious person focuses attention on a sacred artifact—for example, a cross or a Star of David—it functions as a symbol for the experiential gestalt, the connotative feelings and emotions symbolized by the artifact. Paintings or sculptures are frequently viewed within the context of the feelings they arouse, feelings they symbolize for that particular person. The work of art, the old photograph, and the religious artifact are all seen within a contextual background of connotative feelings.

The meaning, then, of an image is determined by the background in which the image is symbolically embedded. This is true whether the background is one of abstract mathematical relationships, linguistically expressed rational understanding, or feelings connotative of that particular image. When a particular person sees the planets in the evening sky, they are viewed within the context of visual imagery plus an understanding as conceived in language. For the ancient Egyptian or the early Hopi Indian, this understanding included supernatural entities, objectifications of their subjective experiences. Their language, being more gestalt in nature, made it relatively easy, I maintain, for such objectifications to enter into their thinking. In contemporary Western culture with its Indo-European language, the planets are viewed within the reasoned context of a solar system, gravity, and the theories of astronomy. Our language, being more linear in nature, predisposes us to think and to conceive in a mode consistent with that of Western science.

Experiencing Strong Feelings

The linear, reasoned world view is firmly in control so long as strong feelings are not experienced. Intense feelings cause one's awareness to shift its focus to the "feeling" experience, to the feelings themselves, or to their symbolic representations. In such cases events are no longer experienced in the ordinary, natural way. Reason, for instance, may dissolve as conscious awareness is flooded with anxiety. If the feelings become too intense, an extraordinary thing happens. As awareness focuses on the image that symbolizes these feelings, it becomes *alive* and breaks away from its structural moorings. It breaks loose from the usual Western concepts of time, cause, and identity, and is seen within a context where events are related through feelings instead of natural laws. Events may appear timeless, as with a religious dance or ceremony, and one's identity becomes fused with others as the structure that separates events and personalities dissolves. In such a case it seems as if conscious awareness is impinged upon by feelings and their symbolic representations.

The "Invasions"

At this point let us return to what James (1903) had to say about "invasions" from the unconscious. I suggest that such phenomena, typical of the "varieties of religious experience," occur when *the meaning of something within awareness shifts from the structure of the world view to the feelings symbol-*

ized by particular image. That is, with "an invasion" from the unconscious an image is no longer seen simply as an unsymbolized form (as a cow or an ape might experience it) or as a symbol within a linguistically structured understanding. Instead, it is experienced primarily as feeling, rather than as an element in a rational structure. The image is *felt* as it reflects its connotative feelings, and expresses in symbolic form the feeling aspect of one's inner life. In such a case awareness lacks the assumptions of time, natural cause, and separateness-of-items-in-the-world, which disrupts what we ordinarily experience as conscious awareness. As an "invasion" from the unconscious proceeds, the image within one's focal awareness becomes primarily a symbol of feelings, and the influence of structured understanding recedes into the background.

The "Wholly Other"

The mind borrows from its sensory experience of the world to express its emotional content in concrete terms, and this practice is basic to a problem that increases with the intensity of one's emotions. That is, because an image can represent both (a) an object in the world that is "outside" of the self and (b) a subjective ("inside") experience that is symbolically expressed by the image, when the gestalt mode is dominant the two may be condensed into a single unity. When subjective feelings are of relatively low intensity, as is the case when experiencing mathematical formulations, the confusion between the "inside" and the "outside" is minimal or nonexistent, as one might expect when the need for expression through the gestalt mode is not present. But as one's emotions and feelings increase, there is an increased need to express those feelings, and the primary means for such an expression is via the gestalt mode and the symbolic use of sensory images. As feelings increase in both number and intensity, there is a tendency for the symbolic image to be charged with life— to be experienced as if it were alive and external to the self. And when especially strong emotional connotations exist, an image symbolizing these feelings can be experienced as *real, lying outside the self, and in the world.* This is the experience described in chapter 3 as "objectification," a phenomenon that seems to occur when emotional experience is especially intense.

As long as feelings are minimal or nonexistent, the world view is dominated by its structure and there is no confusion between "inside" and "outside," between subjective and objective. Whatever feelings are present can simply be felt or included in symbolic form within the structure of the world view. With "invasions" from the unconscious, there is an upsurge of strong feelings that charges a particular image with significance and meaning. In such a case the structure provided by reason and awareness of sensory images recedes and is replaced by increased awareness of the symbolic expression of feelings, values, emotions, and desires.

When very strong feelings are experienced, one's world view can no longer accommodate their symbolic expression within its structure; awareness then shifts to the symbol itself, which is felt rather than perceived. When this occurs the symbols of emotions, values, intentions, desires, and the like are experienced as having a life of their own. In the case of extreme fear associated with the experience of "the sacred," feelings are "objectified" and appear to emanate from an outside presence, from a power that is experienced as "wholly other." Reality is felt rather than perceived or sensed; feelings come to define what is real. Thus, as James pointed out almost a century ago, an "invasion" from the unconscious takes on the appearance something outside ourselves—or as Otto suggested, something "wholly other."

I realize that the analysis begun in chapter 6 and continued through the present chapter has not been easy to grasp, but it is essential to an understanding of how bimodal mental processing and the natural language system relate to the unconscious and to personal religious experience as described by James, Otto, and Eliade. I have tried to formulate a conception of conscious awareness and the unconscious (unconscious awareness) that is based on a synthesis of bimodal mental processing and the symbolic process. I have taken the experience of "the sacred"—what Otto and Eliade call the hallmark of religion—and have tried to understand it in Jamesian terms as an "invasion" from the unconscious. By introducing the unconscious into our thoughts, I have used a term that is more acceptable to science and perhaps more at home in the fields of psychology and psychotherapy. My claim is that the personal religious experience, which is the *sine qua non* of religion in all of its various forms, is a function of the unconscious "invading" conscious awareness, but not the unconscious as traditionally understood.

While the idea of the unconscious has been around for a long time, it had been used without much precision for years before it was grasped by Freud around the turn of the century and developed into its present form. The fomulation I propose is different. It includes the concept of conscious awareness and an understanding of the symbolic process, but perhaps more to the point, this account of the unconscious is grounded on the more fundamental idea that human beings process information in two basic ways: the linear mode and the gestalt mode. This crucial element brings both unconscious and religious phenomena into an arena with the hard sciences. We potentially have a nodal point, the union of certain aspects of psychology (and psychotherapy), religion, and neurology, three ostensibly separate fields. And with such a conjunction we perhaps have the beginning of a synthesis of all three into a unity of thought. It is hoped that psychotherapy can eventually be included within scientific thought. Although this may happen in the distant future, there is always hope that science and religious passion will reinforce one another, human values harmonizing with both the analytical faculty and empirical observations of the world.

Thus far I have outlined a new formulation of the unconscious and have examined its implications for personal religious experience, as described by James and Otto. In chapter 8, I will be less technical, more historical, and perhaps more speculative as I discuss how the integration of one's mental processing leads to a "drive to find God."

8

Perceiving the Whole:
The Human "Drive to Find God"

The time has come to examine the effects of integrating the two modes of mental processing. Does their combination add something that is otherwise missing? Does the whole include more than merely the sum of the parts, something that arises only because the integration takes place? In a sense, conscious awareness itself can be said to be just this sort of phenomenon, but I shall suggest that the integration of the two modes of mental processing introduces another important dimension to both psychology and religion, a motivational state that includes such elements as responsibility and choice. Additionally, I shall maintain that bimodal processing includes a drive to find an ultimate meaning, a drive to find God, as it were. In short, I suggest that the integration of these two modes of processing gives rise to that restless urge in human beings to satisfy their religious needs.

THE DRIVE FOR A COMPLETED GESTALT

Man tries to make for himself in a fashion that suits him best a simplified and intelligible picture of the world: he then tries to some extent to substitute this cosmos of his own for the world of experience, and thus to overcome it. This is what the painter, the poet, and the speculative philosopher, and the natural scientists do, each in their own fashion. Each makes this cosmos and its construction the pivot of his emotional life, in order to find in this way the peace and security that he cannot find within the all-too-narrow realm of swirling personal experiences. . . . (Albert Einstein, from Hoffman 1972, pp. 221–222)

On reading the above passage, one is struck by Einstein's uncanny psychological perceptiveness. In one short, lucid paragraph he intuitively relates the artist, the philosopher, and the natural scientist, and, with extraordinary acumen, he goes directly to the heart of the correlation—namely, the formulation of one's own world or cosmic view and the individual's struggle to find peace and security through his emotional investment in it. Furthermore, Einstein seems to have intuitively perceived that creativity is driven by this need for the peace and security of the completed Gestalt of one's own world view.

When Einstein related the struggle to find peace and security within his own internally created cosmos he was speaking of himself, but undoubtedly he was wise enough to know that this struggle accurately describes humankind generally. He uttered these words in 1918 at an official celebration of Planck's sixtieth birthday. The words were of Planck, but they reveal something of Einstein's passion to find a unified cosmic view. On that occasion Einstein went on to say:

> The supreme task of the physicist is to arrive at those universal elementary laws from which the cosmos can be built up by pure deduction. There is no logical path to these laws; only intuition, resting on sympathetic understanding, can lead to them. . . . The longing to behold (cosmic) harmony is a source of the inexhaustible patience and perseverance with which Planck has devoted himself . . . to the most general problems of our science. . . . The state of mind that enables a man to do work of this kind is akin to that of the religious worshipper or the lover; the daily effort comes from no deliberate intention or program, but straight from the heart. (Hoffman 1972, p. 222)

Again, we are struck by Einstein's extraordinary intuition and his ability to articulate his own "longing to behold (cosmic) harmony" as a source of motivation, and his perception that his creative moments originated less from an effort of consciously willed logic than from an instantaneous and unconscious integration. It is as if Einstein intuitively perceived and poetically articulated the *motivational aspect of the individual's drive for a sense of cosmic harmony, for a consistent world view and a unity of mind.*

Creativity and Bimodal Mental Processing

One thing is clear on reading about Einstein's work and his life: he seemed to have let his idea of the unity of all creation guide his intuition. This view appears to underlie his work on the general theory of relativity as well as his passion to find a unity of electromagnetic forces and matter. For Einstein the principle of "unity" implied a beauty in the symmetry of different aspects of nature, and he marvelled at this unity as he perceived our universe.

Thus, he labored for years to achieve a unity of electromagnetic field and matter, things which were basically of different sorts. While he never achieved this unity to his complete satisfaction, the concept seemed to guide him throughout his life. Indeed, as one biographer puts it: "Einstein, with his feeling of humility, awe, and wonder in a sense of oneness with the universe, belongs with the great religious mystics" (Hoffman 1972, p. 94).

Perhaps it was Einstein's own experience of unity that entered into his conviction that there is oneness in the universe. One morning, after years of futile effort, he awakened and sat up in bed as the pieces to the relativity "puzzle fell into place with an ease and naturalness that gave him an immediate sense of confidence" (Hoffman 1972, p. 69). It was as if he had intuitively perceived a unity in his picture of the cosmos, an integration that had occurred outside of his awareness.

Nor was Einstein alone among the geniuses who perceived intuitively the "whole" of a harmonious mosaic. Poincare, for instance, gave a particularly vivid account of his own experience in this area. He was born some twenty-five years before Einstein and was professor at the University of Paris. When Einstein published the first of his relativity papers, there were only a few men who could understand what he had to say, and Poincare was one of them. He was a man of many facets and his genius spilled over into the field of psychology, for he was very curious about the psychology of discovery. Thus Poincare (1952) described his own personal experience concerning mathematical functions, which had earlier established him among the world's great minds. For fifteen days, he said, he had sat several hours each day at his work table mulling over these functions, to no avail. Then, one evening he drank some black coffee, which was contrary to his usual routine, and he could not sleep. Ideas arose in great abundance. He felt them collide until pairs seem to interlock, making stable combinations, and the next morning he had only to write out the results.

Poincare described other experiences as well in which discoveries occurred to him as if he had suddenly become aware of a meaningful Gestalt or pattern of relations. Intrigued, he hypothesized that on such occasions the correct solution for a problem was selected out of the mass of all possible solutions by what he called the "subliminal self." (This was a term much in use at the time, thanks largely to W. H. F. Myers, a talented psychologist whose theory of the unconscious was eclipsed by Freud.) Poincare suggested that these mathematical solutions were selected by the "subliminal self" on the basis of "mathematical beauty," on the basis of the harmony of members and forms. "It is a real aesthetic feeling which all mathematicians recognize . . . but of which the laymen are so ignorant that they are often tempted to smile at it" (p. 59). Poincare made it clear that he was not talking about some romantic notion of beauty, for he meant, instead, an experience of beauty that comes when the intellect grasps a harmonious mathematical order.

Many of Poincare's contemporaries refused to acknowledge his idea about the preselection of facts, since it seemed to contradict and undermine the validity of the scientific method. For them the principle of objectivity was to observe selected facts and then to build a theory out of the observed data. But Poincare was not alone in his contention that intuition worked by first grasping the "whole." The eminent physicist Maxwell, in the introduction to his *Treatise on Electricity and Magnetism* (1873), compared methods used by Farraday with those current in mathematical physics of the time. The method Farraday used, Maxwell explained, resembled those in which one begins with a "whole" and arrives at the parts only by analysis, while the ordinary procedure depended upon the principle of beginning with parts and building up the whole by synthesis. Maxwell made it clear that he preferred the method of Farraday (Maxwell 1873, pp. 10–21).

Proceeding a step further, the later lectures of Planck, delivered in 1909, as well as the words of Eddington, written in 1923, both suggest that the interplay between the parts of a whole—the processes connecting the elements—is indispensable in understanding the whole and that, indeed, something would be lost if one started only with the individual parts themselves. Planck, for instance, wrote the following:

[W]e think of the wholes before us as the sums of their parts. But this procedure presupposes that the splitting of a whole does not affect the character of the whole. . . . One cannot understand (certain processes he was discussing) on the assumption that all properties of the whole may be approached by the study of its parts. (Plank 1915, pp. 97–98)

Likewise, Eddington (1929) wrote in *The Nature of a Physical World:*

[T]here is one ideal of survey which would look into a very minute compartment of science and turn to see what it may contain and so make what it would regard as a complete inventory of the world. But this misses any world-features which are not located in minute compartments. (p. 103)

There seemed to be an array of eminent scientists who appreciated the fact that to advance in science one had to appreciate the importance of the whole, and that the totality is often quite different from the sum of the parts. These distinguished scholars and theorists were aware that their own intuition was guided by a need to find unity, not only in the physical universe but, more accurately, in their own conceptual world. They appeared to recognize that their intuition was guided by a sense of wholeness that contained a dynamic interplay between the parts, an interplay that would be lost if only the parts themselves were examined. It is as if a significant portion of the scientific community was echoing the Gestalt psychologists. It's tempting to say that these great minds were influenced by Gestalt psychology, but as it happens, some of them—such as Farraday and Maxwell—were writing well before the Gestalt psychologists put pen to paper. Indeed, it is apparent when reading Poincare, Einstein, Eddington, and Planck that they were very much impressed by their own aesthetic sense of unity. Instead of influencing them, the Gestalt psychologists experimentally corroborated their insights.

One last point: the experiences just described graphically demonstrate how the synthetic function of the gestalt mode of processing can in fact integrate *reason,* sensation, and feeling. This is a surprising development but a welcome one because it casts light on the *creative process* that would appear to need a healthy portion of both modes of processing. And it dispels any idea that the gestalt mode of processing is reserved for more primitive or archaic forms of thought.

Two Kinds of Knowing

At this juncture a curious question arises. Is reason driven by intuiting the whole, thereby receiving its power and direction entirely from that gestalt integration? Or can reason function independently of a hidden but intuited Gestalt? In philosophical terms we are dealing with the question of the primacy of intuition or reason, and in religious terms with the classical question of the primacy of faith or reason. In science we are questioning whether advances are made only by explicit rules of logical deduction and inductive generalization, or whether reason receives its power and direction by reaching for some form or hidden meaning. Translated into the terminology we have been using, it becomes a question of whether the linear or the gestalt mode of processing guides our intellectual progress. Are there two kinds of "knowing," one rational and linear, while the other is understood in terms of gestalts and forms?

This is a classical problem, one with which even the philosopher Plato was faced. He argued that the task of solving a problem is logically absurd and therefore impossible.

> If one already knows the solution then there is no need to search for it. And if we do not know the solution then we do not know where to search since we do not know what we are looking for. (Plato as quoted in Polanyi 1974, p. 124)

Polanyi concurred and went on to give further argument for the primacy of "form" over reason.

> The task of solving a problem must indeed appear self-contradictory unless we admit that we can possess true intimations

of the unknown. . . . Plato's argument proves . . . that every advance in understanding is moved and guided by our power for seeing the presence of some hidden comprehensive entity behind . . . clues pointing . . . toward . . . this . . . unknown entity. (And he goes on to state that) all explicit forms of reasoning, whether deductive or inductive, are impotent in themselves; they can operate only as the intellectual tools of man's tacit powers reaching toward the hidden meaning of things. (Polanyi 1974, p. 124)

Another alternative, of course, is that one's perception of the whole is determined and secondary to what one's rational processes have already put together. Thus it could be argued that Einstein's or Poincare's experience of the instantaneous integration of mathematical wholes was not, in fact, possible for the primitives who believed that their comrade was killed by witches, and vice versa. The primitives had no experience of calculus or differential equations but had, instead, constructed a world view of supernatural powers and entities. Einstein had the converse experience, and thus the gestalt integration possible to each was restricted by previous experience.

A third possibility is that these two processes work together creatively and that there is an epigenetic construction such that new possibilities for rational constructs occur with every new gestalt integration, which in turn further illuminates the whole. I prefer this third hypothesis. However, it cannot be contested that there is power in the perception of a completed Gestalt, and I shall argue that it is just such a power that motivates individuals to fulfill their religious needs, that drives them to seek God. But before moving ahead, let us first consider briefly the Gestalt psychologists to whom I have already referred.

Gestalt Psychology

When psychology first began developing as a new science, some one hundred years ago, the study of perception lent itself most readily to experimentation. The members of one group of scientists who studied perception were those whom we now call Gestalt psychologists. Their approach was contrary to the usual methods of traditional scientific inquiry. Instead of beginning their investigations by getting to know the particular facts and then proceeding gradually to examine more and more complex conditions, the Gestalt psychologists approached their research from the opposite direction. They started with raw perceptual experiences and then looked for whatever remarkable facts stood out in the whole of these experiences. For instance, in the visual area Gestalt psychologists found that humans perceive shapes as a "whole," and that individual stimuli or even familiar patterns seem to disappear because they do not stand out. The researchers then compared these observations with other global experiences, trying to isolate the similarities and to suggest general rules that might apply to the "whole."

This reversal of the usual scientific procedure was severely criticized by many of their contemporaries, for psychology was then a young science and it only made sense that this young upstart school should proceed by the established rules before embarking on its own course. Thus the Gestalt psychologists were looked upon with some skepticism by other scientists and by experimental psychologists in particular.

Adding Meaning to One's Life

Through the work of the three primary pioneers of Gestalt psychology, Koffka, Kohler, and Wertheimer, the field gradually developed. One very basic tenant of Gestalt psychology emerged from their work: the way an object is perceived is determined by the total context in which the object is embedded. This relates to the concept of "meaning," particularly the relationship of the world view to the meaning given to life. That is, the meaning one gives to life is defined by the context (world view) in which that life is embedded.

A second principle of Gestalt psychology is that the whole is greater than the sum of the parts. The interaction of the component parts adds a new dimension to the whole that is not present until the parts are combined. This, too, is important for our discussion because it emphasizes the interaction between the various parts of our mental processing, which I will maintain is important both in conscious awareness and as a motivational factor in human behavior.

> The decisive question for man is: is he related to something infinite or not? That is the telling question of his life. Only if we know that the thing which truly matters is the infinite can we avoid fixing our interests upon futilities and upon all kinds of goals which are not of real importance. (Jung 1963, p. 325)

The meaning for our respective lives comes through intuiting our relationship with something larger than ourselves, the "whole" of a world view of which we are a part. If we feel a part of a particular country, race, team, or company, for instance, then our perspective does not "truly matter," for we will fix goals for ourselves that are "not of real importance." Consider the case in which a person's primary concern derives from being a member of the KKK, where he derives the direction for his behavior and the meaning for his life from the role he plays in the activities of that organization. Certainly this individual is ruled by different guidelines than someone who identifies most strongly with the human race. Alternatively, when personal identity depends upon participation in certain economic circles, the main concern might be money or economic power, whereas if identity and personal meaning revolves around family, then the person's main concern will be oriented toward personal relationships, family unity, keeping to family tradition, and the like. The point here is that what becomes a person's main concern—the "ultimate concern"—is a reflection of the meaning that that person finds in his own life, which is to say it is a function of the world or cosmic view in which the individual conceives himself (herself) to be embedded. For Jung, it is only when individuals see themselves in relation to the infinite, when the "whole" of which they are a part is something infinite, that they find a meaning to life that is of "real importance."

I am of course extrapolating from the early gestalt experiments with sensory perception and using their thesis as it might apply to the total experience of the individual. While this might lack experimental rigor, I feel justified in trying to see an individual's life experience as a "whole," and I suggest that the basic process of integration examined by the Gestalt psychologists in the sensory area applies to the person's entire life experience. I further suggest that each of us *must* complete our own world view and make it internally consistent, including the subjective aspects, as discussed in the previous chapters.

In addition to being endowed with a superior neural network and a superior faculty for symbolizing, *human beings have been presented with the imperative to find meaning.* It would seem that as long as inconsistency or incompleteness exist in the individual's world view, his mind will search to round it out with a coherent conception of meaning. However, the human gift for symbolizing and conceptualizing, and the accompanying ability to find meaningful forms among the swirl of data and information available, brings with it a liability. Along with an ability to find symbolic meanings, the individual human is also susceptible to disillusionment, boredom, depression, and despair. It would appear that with such extraordinary cerebral endowment, humans have the "honor" of being the only living creatures capable of such anguish.

COGNITIVE DISSONANCE AND MOTIVATION

The second point about Gestalt psychology that relates to our present discussion has to do with the interplay of the parts of the whole, which brings us back to the discussion concerning the interplay between the different modes of mental processing. Lewin, an associate of Wertheimer and Kohler at the University of Berlin in the years following World War I, applied these concepts to individuals in their environment and to sociological phenomena, and in so doing he became a leading proponent of what is called "field theory," as it applies to psychology. Here the basic principle is essentially that behavior is the function of the field in which it exists at the time it occurs. Lewin's thought and theory represents an extension of Gestalt principles into the personal and interpersonal scene. He made certain observations that, along with others, influenced Festinger (1957) to define a psychological state that he called *cognitive dissonance.* According to Festinger, this is a *"motivational state" that arises from inconsistent knowledge, a state that impels the individual to attempt to reduce or to eliminate the inconsistency.* If, for instance, a fearful person cannot find an adequate cause for fear, then the knowledge of the fear is inconsistent with the knowledge that there is nothing to fear. According to cognitive dissonance theory, the individual is motivated to either reduce the fear or to find some provoking event. Furthermore, individuals can do this in any one of three ways. (1) We can misperceive or misinterpret the environment and, in this case, see it as threatening when in reality it is not—as when a tone of voice is misinterpreted as angry when it is intended to be sympathetic or merely "matter of fact." (2) Through our actions we can induce the world to treat us in a way that is consistent with our feelings—as when someone who is paranoid behaves in a defensive and angry way and induces others to respond in like manner. Or (3) we can change our own logical constructs and internal feeling states to become consistent with reality; in this case we no longer feel afraid. This, in effect, is what psychotherapy is all about: the therapist helps the patient do (3) instead of (1) and (2) and thus to rid the client of bad feelings and destructive behaviors.

Let me point out that if the word "cognitive" sounds too restrictive, it should be understood to include not only what we usually think of as "cognitive processes"—thinking in words, reasoning in sentences, and the like—but also "any bit of knowledge that a person has about himself or the environment" (Wicklund & Brehm 1976, p. 2). Such knowledge would include valuing and believing as well as an awareness of feelings, memories, intentions, and so on. Any knowledge that individuals have about themselves or the environment is a "cognition," or "cognitive element." These cognitions would include such information as nationality, height, weight, memory of previous events, an intent to go to work the next day, personal knowledge of feeling states, and (it seems to me) even "knowledge" (belief) about what is right and wrong. Cognitions pertaining to the environment would include such things as the knowledge of the distance between Atlanta and New Orleans; the fact that the sky is blue and the grass is green; the fact that one's car needs a tune-up; and even (it seems to me) the "knowledge" (belief) of the relativity theory or of the Copernican theory of planetary movement, the "knowledge" (belief) that angels hold the stars in their place in the heavens, the belief that the earth is in the center of the universe because God placed man on the central and most important planet, the belief that a medicine man can place a hex on someone and kill them, and the belief that the great sky beetle (Khepra) appears self-created each day to roll the sun across the sky.

If two cognitive elements are consonant, then they apply to one another in some psychological sense. Knowing that ice cream tastes good is consonant with the idea of eating ice cream. A relationship between two cognitive elements is dissonant, however, where the person has cognitions of one sort coexisting with other cognitions that imply the opposite. If a person believes a particular political figure to be a crook and yet votes for that individual, then the two cognitions are in a dissonant relationship. Knowing the earth to be a rather small planet that circles an insignificant sun on the periphery of the Milky Way is dissonant with the idea that because humankind is created in God's own image, God placed humans on *terra firma* in the center of the universe.

Knowing that the myth of three magi visiting the virgin birth of a savior god existed in the Middle East long before the time of Jesus is dissonant with the literal interpretation of the Bible (Smith 1952).

Choice, Behavioral Commitment, and Personal Responsibility

In addition to the motivating aspects, the theory of cognitive dissonance has also been expanded to include such concepts as choice, behavioral commitment, and the sense of personal responsibility, all of which have moral implications. There is, for instance, an argument here for living in accordance with one's stated ethical ideals. Believing that it is right for others to be truthful in their dealings with us is consonant with reciprocal behavior on our part. According to cognitive dissonance theory, there are real consequences to ethical consistency and an argument in favor of consistency as a standard by which something can be judged "good" or "bad."

Brehm and Cohen (1962) emphasized the importance of behavioral commitment, suggesting that when a person commits himself to an attitudinal or behavioral act, then the corresponding cognitions are highly resistant to change. Furthermore, research has suggested that personal responsibility and choice are also involved in increasing or reducing motivation. Thus, an awareness of this motivational state gives insights into the importance of ethics, responsibility, and choice in daily life—a fact that relates to religion, psychotherapy, and clinical psychology.

Gestalt psychology, Lewin's field theory, and the newer discipline of cognitive dissonance share more than their mutual historical influence upon one another. They emphasize the "whole" and the importance of the dynamic interaction of the component parts on the whole. All this is pertinent to my discussion because I am suggesting the importance of a *mental* unity or whole, a unity of reason and feeling, and a unity of the two modes of mental processing through which these experiences are expressed in symbolic form. Furthermore, I am suggesting a motivational aspect to the integration of these processes. When incompleteness or inconsistency invades a person's world view—it is focused on structure, feeling aspects, or elements of both—the individual is motivated to seek out and correct the inconsistencies.

What I am suggesting is of course more inclusive than that which is covered in cognitive dissonance theory. However, there is an interesting historical fact suggesting that scientists in this area might not object too strenuously. As chance would have it, one of the closest personal friends of Gazzaniga, a pioneer in the split-brain research, is Festinger who, as already mentioned, published the seminal work that initially established the field of cognitive dissonance. Undoubtedly influenced by Festinger, Gazzaniga has suggested that the theory of cognitive dissonance can be integrated into the theoretical ideas generated by the split-brain research (Gazzaniga & LeDoux 1978, Gazzaniga 1985). If the importance of an idea is established by its consonance with seemingly unrelated ideas, then perhaps the workers in this area may welcome our thoughts, for their ideas are generally compatible with what I have said about symbolism, meaning, conscious awareness, the unconscious, and the two modes of mental processing. Their emphasis on such areas as choice, responsibility, commitment, and a unity of cognitive factors is not only consistent with our ideas but can be incorporated into our own position.

For the first time we can begin to understand in a naturalistic way what motivates and moves human beings in their restless and relentless pursuit for completeness, the drive to complete the Gestalt of their world views. It is this that propels humans in their search to fill gaps in their knowledge, in their search for explanations, and their need for both theistic and naturalistic formulations about the nature of things. And it is this that has lent so much power to both religious and scientific pursuits. We can now begin to examine the human striving for completeness and the need for a consistent belief system using natural rather than supernatural terms, as well as the drive to complete their science.

THE "DRIVE" TO FIND GOD

The behavioral psychologists have taught us to distinguish between variables that direct behavior and those that "energize" an organism's behavior, a difference analogous to that between the steering mechanism and the engine of a car (Hebb 1955). The degree of activation and vigor with which an organism is motivated is thought of as "drive," and the behaviorists have conceived of such drives as energizing organisms to seek out food, water, and sexual satisfaction.

Humanity certainly shares with its animal cousins the motivation to seek food, water, and sex; but in addition there seems to be an additional motivating factor, a need for the completeness and consistency of personal world views. Certainly we all do not perceive the mathematical wholeness of the theory of relativity, but like Einstein we all need to perceive a wholeness in our own experiential cosmos.

Basic to this thesis is the idea that there are different

modes of mental processing, and I suggest here that when they do not work in concert the organism is "driven" to reduce the discrepancies. This applies on several levels. When dissonance occurs in the rational (linear) data there is a need for the individual to reduce the inconsistency and to harmonize the parts into a rational whole. One need only refer to the experiences of Einstein and Poincare for pertinent examples. The same can be said of the feelings we experience. In addition, there is a need for internal consistency between values and behavior. At the same time, when there is a dissonance or a lack of harmony between feelings and reason—i.e., when there is an inconsistency between feelings, as symbolized by the gestalt mode, and reason, as symbolized by the linear mode—the individual is motivated to reduce the discrepancy.

As such, human beings are motivated by any incompleteness or inconsistency in their world view to reject whatever "fact" or feeling that cannot be integrated, be it observational/ rational and thus relatively structured, or more emotional and feeling in nature. (The ultimate experience of incompleteness is, of course, that experience which religion is forever preoccupied, the recognition of one's own finite existence and one's own impending death. Becker, in his truly remarkable book *The Denial of Death,* has eloquently discussed the various ways individuals try to come to terms with the fear of death, the ultimate incompleteness.)

I suggest that this incompleteness is experienced as a "longing to behold (cosmic) harmony" and as a generalized anxiety or vague uneasiness that spurs us on in the search for unity. We are motivated to seek out, to act, and to rationalize and adjust our belief system. This is what impels human beings to formulate what James (1903) calls "over beliefs," the religious doctrines and dogmas that try to make values and feelings consistent with a matrix of reason. This incompleteness is what the individual feels when searching for meaning and value in life; it is the subjective experience of the person's "drive to find God." It propels the individual in the quest for faith, in the quest for a complete and consistent belief system, and it is what impels humanity down the path of theology, philosophy, and science.

In my discussion of the two kinds of knowing, I suggested that humans are influenced by a need to search out the reasoned constituents of an intuited meaning. It should be pointed out that the universe seems to contain in its organization a hierarchy of meanings that theoretically leads to an ultimate meaning, i.e., the meaning of the cosmos as a whole. It would likewise seem that humankind, in its restless quest for a greater and greater understanding, seems to be searching for this ultimate understanding and meaning. And while the individual uses reason to analyze his perception of the "whole," reason itself is stretching for something greater, an intuited whole beyond the perceived particulars. This passionate pursuit of meaning suggests that the individual is "driven" to find unity and to grasp the entirety of his subjective experience, i.e., his perceptual image and his reason, and the structure each reflects. Added to this unity are the person's emotions, values, desires, intentions, etc. He is driven to find an ultimate meaning in the integration of self and cosmos. Indeed, I speculate that *there exists in the individual a "drive" to find an ultimate in meaning, a drive to find God.*

9

Science, Feelings, and Psychiatry

The cause and effect relationship from physiology to feelings is not a one-way street; subjective experiences also affect physiology—witness the examples of voodoo death. To go one important step further, subjective experience itself is changed through subjective means, something we see in both religion and psychotherapy. But so far we have not satisfactorily included within psychology such phenomena as voodoo death or the processes and effects of psychotherapy and religious experience. A complete psychology—a complete science of mind—must account for such phenomena. It must include an understanding of "believing" as a powerful influence in human existence, and our present discussion, or something very much like it, is needed as a beginning step toward a more complete understanding of the human being.

I have attempted to look at (certain aspects of) magical beliefs and religious experience from a psychological perspective, and, in so doing, extend the conceptual world of psychology to include those aspects of the human being that

191

do not present themselves in a logical, rational form. The question naturally arises as to how this might be done while at the same time complying with the demands of science that its theoretical constructs be tested against objective fact. How can feelings be tested against fact when they are not experienced as objects and do not present themselves in the linear form of reason?

I contend that one answer to this question is to first establish through conventional experimental research the basic modes used by the human mind to organize data, and then to see how aspects of subjective experience might be formulated as functions of these modes of organization. More specifically, the approach here is to examine how (aspects of) magical beliefs and religious experience might be understood as functions of bimodal mental processing. This is not an argument by analogy since the way the mind organizes experience is a common denominator of all human mental life, from the awareness of a test situation in a split-brain experiment to the awareness of the experience of "the sacred." Both are psychological experiences and fall within the same conceptual category.

At this juncture, it might be useful to point out that, ideally, the science of psychology not only observes nature and forms a rational understanding from its observations, but it also allows for a predictability and usefulness in its dealings with nature. But where are we to find usefulness and predictability when dealing purely with the feeling aspect of subjective experience? Where can we hope to find usefulness and predictability when we are attempting to capture such elusive quarry: How does subjective experience influence subjective experience? How does a change in belief relate to a change in values, intentions, desires, etc.?

One place to look is in the area of clinical psychiatry in general and psychotherapy in particular, two of psychology's important representatives in the arena of practical application. If there is validity in the idea that aspects of religious experience and magical beliefs can be viewed as functions of bimodal mental processing, the symbolic process, and the unconscious, then we should see that neurotic and psychotic symptomatology as well as the therapeutic process itself can also be formulated as functions of these same concepts. Care must be taken not to misread this, for *I certainly am not equating religious phenomena with neurotic or psychotic symptomatology.* I am merely saying that these formulations should allow an understanding of both areas. (Artistic expression can likewise be viewed as an expression of the unconscious, but it does not need to be seen as pathological, psychotic, neurotic, or inferior in any way. Instead, artistic expression can be seen as the human mind's attempt to find symbolic expression in objective forms, as objectifications or products of the process of objectification. Likewise, various aspects of religious expression can be seen in a similar way, as the human mind's stretching to express itself as "symbolic forms," as Cassirer suggested long ago.) If these ideas prove useful in psychiatry or psychotherapy and lead to some type of predictability in the therapeutic situation or in understanding mental illness, then we have the very thing we seek. The point is, if the concept of bimodal mental processing has validity for understanding the phenomena of psychiatry and psychotherapy, then support is gained for the thesis that aspects of religious experience and magical beliefs can be understood in the same terms. Let us therefore turn to consider how these ideas about symbolism and bimodal mental processing might relate to psychotherapy and psychiatry in general.

PSYCHODYNAMIC AND
PSYCHOTHERAPEUTIC
CONSIDERATIONS

The clinical vignettes presented earlier in this book hint that various aspects of psychotherapy might well be understood in terms of bimodal mental processing. Whereas other theoretical formulations might do just as well, it would seem that the more fundamental approach is to start with how the human mind organizes data. Thus, the idea of bimodal mental processing would seem not only to be more basic but the ground upon which other legitimate formulations are built. Let us at this point give further consideration to how bimodal mental processing relates to psychiatry and psychotherapy, with especial emphasis on how it might relate to what we know of the symbolic process.

Because images serving as gestalt symbols are so much more evocative of emotional responses than words arranged into sentences or paragraphs, such images can be used in therapy to help a patient become aware of feelings. Ferenczi (1926) used this observation in dealing with obsessional patients when he asked them to visualize memories and fantasies. More recently, in gestalt therapy the visualization of feelings as an image, or the "reliving" of past experiences by visualizing them in the mind's eye, serves the same purpose, i.e., helping the patient confront the full intensity of his or her feelings.

Anxiety, erotic feelings, and anger can be activated by images; Jones (1929) pointed out that such an activation is used defensively by patients in therapy. In other words, when confronted with something threatening they may use such images to evoke other, emotionally laden experiences to consume their attention rather than confront the more threatening material. Horowitz (1972) echoed this point, suggesting that the psychoanalyst is particularly interested in the clinical situation that occurs when a patient's mind shifts from words to images—for instance, a male patient whose free associations lead him to verbalize a homosexual attraction for the therapist. The patient might interrupt himself with a sexual fantasy about a naked woman, since the erotic feelings elicited by this fantasy are more acceptable than the thought of his homosexual attractions. Horowitz's formulations were somewhat different from those presented here, but his thoughts are pertinent to anyone interested in the integration of psychodynamic considerations with bimodal mental processing.

Another point of therapeutic interest has been made by Galin (1974), who commented on how material presented to a patient might be handled differently depending on whether it is encountered in a linear or a gestalt form. He speculated on the difficulties a child might have, for example, in processing conflicting messages from a mother: one a verbal (linear) message that says, "I love you, dear," while the nonverbal facial (gestalt) expression says, "I hate you" or "I will hurt you." Conceivably, one part of the mind-brain dyad will attend to the verbal cues because it cannot handle information from the facial expression very well, while a second part attends to the nonverbal cues because it does not easily understand words. (It seems conceivable to picture the conscious awareness of the mother talking to its counterpart in the child, while at the same time the mother's unconscious communicates with the child's unconscious—a speculative but intriguing thought.)

The Reciprocal Inhibition of Structure and Emotions

One of the fascinating aspects of these ideas concerning information processing has to do with a reciprocal inhibition between the emotional and the structural aspects of one's subjective experience. In the previous discussion of the primitives' beliefs, I discussed the situation in which a native was killed by a shark. We saw that the poor victim's comrades, overcome with anxiety, "explained" the death in terms of witches and magical forces, objectifications of their intense feelings. In the primitives' world, when an emotionally charged event occurs (in this case a death), the reasoned and structural aspect of their experience recedes into the background, and the influence of emotions on their sense of reality is greatly enhanced.

No matter how much we would like to deny our own similarity to those primitive natives, we have all experienced this same inhibitive effect between feelings and structure when a flood of anxiety causes a temporary lapse of reason and memory. The inverse is also the case, for it seems that an increased awareness of the structure of reality diminishes the emotional aspect of an experience. The extreme example of this is our experience of mathematics, where the emotional content is perhaps entirely missing. In psychotherapy this reciprocal inhibitive effect is used when patients are encouraged to be "more rational" at times of emotional turmoil.

A skilled psychotherapist sees these phenomena daily as patients struggle with emotionally charged issues. An example of this was given earlier in chapter 5 in the discussion of the patient Carol. Another patient who exhibited this was a thirty-two-year-old engineer, Jerry C., who had come to therapy originally to curb outbursts of temper and to overcome his general difficulty in relating to individuals who are important to him. He had been in therapy about six months when he made the following remarks during a therapy session.

When I get angry it's like something comes over me, and it's like I'm someone else. I don't think. I don't think about anything. I just feel angry. Sometimes I don't even remember what I've said.

It was about the same point in therapy that Jerry described how he felt when others around him became angry or started to pout. He said he felt anxious and had difficulty separating himself from them. He described his feelings in the following:

It's hard for me to know what to do. . . . It's hard to pull myself out of the situation. . . . It's like I'm a little child. . . . I don't feel separate from the outside world. It's like I'm just in this big ball. . . . If I'm in a room with my father or my girlfriend and they are angry. I feel I'm a part of or cause of the anger. It's as if I'm the center of the goddamn universe, thinking of it now, but not at the time. I'm part of it at the time.

It's hard to separate all that out. The bottom line is that I don't feel I have a choice. I feel I'm part of it (and) I do this in every situation I can think of, with my father, with my kids, with R. (his girlfriend). *Actually I was not aware of all this until right at this moment, as I am talking about it right now.*

How the "Talking Therapy" Works

The above mentioned quotation is meant to demonstrate the difficulty Jerry had in separating himself from others when he felt strong emotions. But just as important for our purposes is Jerry's description of the therapeutic effect of translating his feelings into words, a process that helped him become consciously aware of feelings that previously he had only vaguely felt. After putting his experience into words and becoming consciously aware of what he was doing, Jerry slowly learned how to separate himself from others. The therapeutic effect of "just talking" is seen repeatedly in psychotherapy, although most patients are not so clear in articulating the fact that this translation of feelings into words actually helps them become aware and to change.

All this relates to one of the most exciting aspects of these ideas, i.e., the question of why the "talking therapy" works. In the course of our investigation, much has been said about the role of language (which, of course, happens to be the "tool" of psychotherapy) and how it relates to both conscious awareness and the unconscious. The theory presented here suggests an understanding of how "talking" relates to conscious awareness and thus an understanding of the axiom—repeated by many of the giants in the field—that psychotherapy consists of "making the unconscious conscious," i.e., the patient becoming consciously aware of that which he (or she) was previously unaware. By translating his feelings into words and sentences, Jerry translated his feelings into a more structured and stable form, a form more accessible to conscious awareness.

Jerry's words clearly articulated the fact that expressing his feelings allowed him to better separate himself from others. It was as if either his feelings or his reasoning powers had exclusive control of his awareness, and when his anger (or fear) was strong enough, it took precedence. Overpowered by strong feelings of anger, Jerry's ability to separate and discriminate (characteristic of the linear mode) faded into the background. Within the therapeutic situation, the patient was able to translate his vivid feelings into words and thus become aware of that part of himself which had previously been little more than a vague feeling. And as he did so it strengthened his sense of self, his personal power, and his feeling of control over his own mental processes. Over time Jerry gained a sense of responsibility for what was happening within himself, and his behavior and self-control gradually improved. The patient developed a clearer sense of integration, of being the same person whether or not he was angry.

Perhaps one of the fortuitous benefits of formulating conscious awareness and the unconscious in terms of language will be to understand psychotherapy within a context acceptable to science. Even those in the "hard" sciences may one day understand how the "talking therapy" works, and then perhaps the prejudice against it in today's "rational, scientific" world will subside.

Neurotic Conflicts

We witnessed in chapter 5 the example of Ralph B., a young man whose neurosis manifested itself in the belief that he was possessed by a demon. This demon was a symbol for the whole of Ralph's "experiential gestalt"—the "inside" feelings of anger that sought to punish him, combined with his fear of being punished, and the "outside" cause, i.e., both the culturally learned image of a demon and his own privately experienced trauma with his father. The demon resolved a dilemma as well, for it relieved Ralph of responsibility for his own unacceptable desires and behaviors. His dystonic feelings were symbolized in the form of a witch, a symbolic gestalt integration of the numerous facets of a wholistic experience. That is, because of the synthetic function of the gestalt mode, where all elements are brought into a whole, we have insight into why a neurotic symptom is said to represent both sides of a conflict. (How there comes to be a conflict in the first place is a different matter. Certainly there is a conflict as to how the two modes of processing would handle information, and thus a "neurotic" conflict on one level can arise because of competition over which "system" (which of the two modes) controls one's experiential sense of reality. And while a conflict may arise over which "system" controls one's sense of reality, a further conflict can result from conflicting "input" into a system: for example, the conflict of a child whose parents tell him not to do something but are observed doing it themselves. Traditional, dynamic psychotherapeutic formulations account for the conflicting input quite well, this new formulation seems to do a better job of deciphering which system is controlling.)

Chapter 5 also presented us with the words of Carol A., a young woman, a modern-day personification of the primitive, who was having difficulty separating her own identity from that of her family. Her family members, who had influenced her thinking to a large degree, showed evidence of an inability to separate themselves individually from one another. They believed that "bad thoughts" or actions brought about punishment, and good thoughts or rituals could protect family members. In short, we saw a demonstration of a lack of separation between family members; Carol herself had never really become "individuated." These concepts find acceptance in a psychotherapeutic practice and can be seen as related to a predominance of the gestalt mode in this family's mental processing.

Furthermore, we saw the example of Mary D., the young professional woman who, in an effort to separate herself from me (her therapist), had tried to burn me in effigy. In a clay pot she cremated a collection of old tissues and statements from my office as she tried to rid herself of the feeling of being "fused" with me. Then she arrived unannounced at my office a few days later to touch me, to reassure herself that I was still alive.

These are examples of magical thinking occurring in psychiatric patients—magical thinking and believing blatantly similar to the magical beliefs of primitives—a very intriguing development to say the least. But even more intriguing is the fact that we can see the same thing in the so-called "normal" population, if we care to look.

Dreams

The lack of structure observed in primitives and in psychiatric patients with neurotic symptoms is evident in all of us. Perhaps it can best be appreciated in that confusing, hectic, emotionally laden, and colorful world of our dreams. The dream state offers minimal influence of structure and maximum latitude to the emotions. In our dream life we focus our awareness on images that serve as symbols, which *are* themselves (in a sense) emotions and subjective experience. Because the dream state lacks linear structure and the distinction between symbols characteristic of the gestalt mode of processing, we find fears and desires serving as causative agents, the condensation of several images into a single element, the part standing for the whole, and the absence of time as an ordering principle. All of these mental functions are the ways we relate elements in our awareness when the influence of structure recedes and the influence of feelings comes to the fore. Aside from the curious fact that these phenomena are the same as those characteristics used to describe primitive beliefs, there is the equally important fact that these are essentially what Freud described as characteristic of unconscious thought processes, an important point that bolsters the credit of his observations at a time when his influence has begun to erode.

Other Psychotherapeutic Implications

The theory formulated here seems to have implications both for the "rational" as well as the "experiential" therapies, since we are dealing with reason and feelings. Transactional analysis and the cognitive therapies, with their emphasis on the rational approach to various inter- and intrapersonal transactions, fall within the former; gestalt therapy, a la Perls (1971), fits within the latter. I have yet to mention the implications of bimodal processing for those psychoanalytic theoreticians interested in object relations. After all, when I speak of symbolic images I am talking about what the psychoanalysts call internalized objects, and when I speak of adifferentiation—a concept that arose out of a consideration of the religious leaders being unable to differentiate a symbol from that for which the symbol stands—I am speaking of a process that describes the inability to separate "self objects" from internalized objects of the world, much like the infant who is unable to separate itself from its mother's nipple. Another example might be that of a borderline patient who is unable to combine the image of a "good mother" with that of a "bad mother"; the patient is having difficulty combining contradictory images or "experiential gestalts."

Additionally, in light of all that has been said, the possible correlation with Jungian psychology seems quite exciting. The idea of animated symbols of gestalt integration reflects a position not far removed from Jung's archetypes. Certainly the fact that Jung emphasized the importance of symbols and developed a more "religiously oriented" psychology than his predecessors, suggests that there may in fact be some concordance between a Jungian view and the views presented here. His dealing with complexes and archetypes as symbolic (gestalt) integrations of the psyche, living and capable of influencing or even dominating one's life and behavior, relates to what has been said here. We might differ with regard to just what "living" means and to what extent the images transcend the material world, but there is a great deal of basic agreement between the concepts. The idea of the individuation of the self as well as the Jungian concept of the self as a (gestalt) integration of various aspects, even conflicting aspects, of the psyche is likewise consistent with the present ideas. Jung developed his theory of symbols to a far greater extent than anything presented here, and such ideas as the therapeutic implications of symbols or the power of numinous symbols excite the imagination with possibilities, but at this point such possibilities are only touched upon. Obviously, more needs to be said about how the ideas I have presented apply to Jungian psychology as well as to other psychotherapeutic formulations, but the implication is clear that combining of the concepts of symbolism and bimodal mental processing has many implications for psychotherapeutic theory, a rather curious and exciting development to be sure.

Because the bimodal theory incorporates the theory of cognitive dissonance, it opens even further possibilities for therapeutic paradigms. I suggested, for instance, that therapy, in essence, can be seen from one perspective as the therapist's attempt to help patients change themselves as opposed to misinterpreting reality or inducing the world to treat them in a pathological way consistent with their own distorted views. The area of cognitive dissonance opens up for psychotherapy a vast array of existential issues related to choice, responsibility, and behavioral commitment—issues that are very much alive and relevant to psychotherapy, but heretofore not successfully integrated into a theory of mind.

UNITY OF THOUGHT WITHIN PSYCHIATRY

Can cerebral asymmetries provide an understanding of clinical syndromes within the psychiatric setting, and, if so, can a psychiatric taxonomy be developed based on this concept? Until only a few years ago this seemed a viable possibility and was discussed as such in the literature (Galin 1974, Wexler & Heninger 1979, Wexler 1980, Gruzelier 1981, Mandell 1985). There have been studies exploring the possibility of cerebral asymmetries in schizophrenia (Gur 1976, 1977; Beaumont & Dimond 1973, Roemer et al. 1978), and in depressive and manic depressive disorders (Gruzelier & Venables 1974; Foucault 1973; d'Elia & Perris 1973, 1974; Myslobodsky & Horesh 1978), as well as studies exploring dysfunction of conduction between the hemispheres (Beaumont & Dimond 1973, Wexler & Heninger 1979, Green 1978). Additionally, it has been shown that there are enzematic differences between the hemispheres, e.g., differences with regard to neurotransmitter agents (Glick et al. 1977, Nieoullon et al. 1978, Mandell 1985). And there have been studies of possible correlations of hemispheric differences and coping strategies (Gainotti 1969, Hecaen & de Ajuriaguerra 1964, Alema et al. 1961, Rossi & Rosadini 1967, Milner 1967).

The picture, however, seems more complicated today than it did just a few years ago, and now it is apparent that the left/right orientation to brain dysfunction is an oversimplification. Instead, one must consider *intra*hemispheric dysfunction in addition to interhemispheric factors (Gruzelier 1981, Gardner 1983, Gazzaniga 1985, Wexler 1988, Galin 1988). Not only must the dysfunction of regions of the brain be considered, but the functional balance between various brain regions must be taken into account: left/right, medial/lateral, anterior/posterior, subcortical/cortical, and so on. In the future it is hoped that there will be a correlation of clinical syndromes with regional brain dysfunctions, but the progress of research and the accumulation knowledge in this area is expanding exponentially, with the theory still in a state of flux. Whereas, for instance, only a few years ago it was suggested that schizophrenia was associated with left-hemisphere dysfunction and depression with right-hemisphere dysfunction, in the present state of research, things are not so clearly dichotomized.

Even with all these reservations there still exists the exciting and extraordinary possibility of eventually uniting biological psychiatry and psychodynamic psychotherapy within the same theoretical framework. Certainly Freud's "Project for a Scientific Psychology" (1954) was an attempt to do this, but he had to abandon his effort when he failed to integrate his psychodynamic formulations with neurophysiology and neuroanatomy in a reasonable fashion. But now that the potential exists for acquiring the means of understanding psychiatric phenomena in terms of dysfunctional regions of the brain or dysfunctional balances between regions, the possibility of a unity within psychiatric thought arises again, something that is sorely needed and whose time must come if the psychodynamic approach to therapy is to be both viable and respectable.

CONCLUSION

Just how can this theory of bimodal processing be of practical use to us? It may be useful in the sense that it can shed new light on such phenomena as religious conversion, the "faith state," obedience to authority, and the like. Perhaps it may even lead to the discovery of physiological (e.g., enzematic) correlations to such experiences or to meditative states and "peak experiences." In addition, it could have practical use and predictive power in psychiatry and psychotherapy. It offers the potential for a new classification of psychiatric disorders based on anatomical and physiological considerations as opposed to the purely descriptive distinctions we have now. If so, there is also the possibility that psychodynamic formulations can be made consistent with neuroanatomy and neurophysiology. Bimodal processing could be useful in examining and understanding the magical thinking of children and the relationship of this thinking to maturation of certain areas of their central nervous systems. It may lead to the development of new techniques or new approaches to psychotherapy. The relationship between linear and gestalt processing could be useful if it illucidates why a particular technique is therapeutic, or if it sheds light on why "just talking" leads to "making the unconscious conscious." A therapist working with a particular patient could use the theory to develop an understanding of the patient and the therapeutic transactions; the therapist might come to understand better the lack of differentiation between a patient and her family or the phenomena of dreams. The theory of bimodal processing could be useful because it provides a rational understanding that includes various psychologies or therapeutic approaches within the same framework—psychologies or approaches that otherwise might be viewed as conflicting. This would be the case, for instance, if it helps therapists to recognize the truths behind both the Freudian and the Jungian perspectives and the more basic ground from which they both arise.

Perhaps it might sound reductionistic to say that so many and such varied aspects of psychotherapy and psychiatric phenomena, as well as aspects of religious experience and magical beliefs, can be viewed as functions of the linear and the gestalt modes of processing. But if these two modes of processing information are in fact the primary ways that the mind organizes experience, then this is just what one would expect!

The focus of this book has been on bimodal mental processing, the concept of symbolism, and how certain religious phenomena might be understood in these terms. Consequently, in order to remain within the intended scope of this discussion, I have only given hints and suggestions as to how these terms might help us understand psychiatric, psychological, and psychotherapeutic phenomena. Much more needs to be clarified, especially regarding the anatomical correlations of the two modes of mental processing, since the left/right distinction undoubtedly is an oversimplification. Time will tell. I submit, however, that there is ample reason to look for predictability and usefulness within the fields of psychiatry and psychotherapy to support the major thesis of this book. That is, there is ample reason to accept that the concepts of bimodal mental processing and the symbolic process can be generative ideas for rationally understanding subjective experience, including magical beliefs and certain aspects of religious experience.

But, it might be questioned, this was supposed to be a discussion primarily about religious experience, and here you are talking about psychiatry and psychotherapy! What is the connection? A good question, I would reply, for it underscores the fact that there is an overlapping of the interests of religion, psychiatry, and psychotherapy, and this allows for one last point to be made.

As has already been stated, both psychotherapy and religious experience exhibit phenomena theoretically related to the unconscious, but in addition both are concerned with "the good life." Both are related to values, happiness, interpersonal relationships, the effects of such emotions as hate and love, self-esteem, feelings of worth and acceptance, and so on. Thus, psychology and psychotherapy provide potential avenues for science to explore various areas that are also of interest to religion. At present, without much acknowledgment of what they are doing, psychology and religion seem generally to be using two different sets of terms to describe human subjective life, with words like *mind, emotion, egostate,* and the like being used by psychologists, while terms such as *faith, spiritual, revelation, soul, salvation,* and so forth are traditionally employed by religious leaders. Suffice it to say that either set of terms can be used, but in doing so we must accept the assumptions that go along with whatever set is chosen; assumptions of a supernatural nature accompany the religious terms, while the psychological terms assume a "natural" course of events. (Certainly any science, including psychology, inherently has more subjective assumptions than was acknowledged before the ideas of such men as Polanyi and Kuhn; but even so, it makes sense to consider the *apparent* differences between science and religion. Differences in appearance are differences.) At present, terms like *soul* and *self* are generally employed without precisely distinguishing their use; and while the psychological terms do not preclude the validity of religious ones, if science is to extend itself into those areas previously left to religion, psychology must restrict itself to its own "natural" viewpoint. The examination of such differences—those between the meanings of the two sets of terms—is important for psychology; and in this volume I have tried to examine more precisely what is meant psychologically by such terms as *holiness, spirit, demons,* and the like.

In conclusion, this chapter has been concerned with practicality, predictability, and how both might be included within a discussion of bimodal mental processing, the symbolic process, and religious experience. The interests of psychology and psychiatry overlap those of religion, and the demonstration that these concepts are relevant for the former provides support for their applicability to the latter. If it withstands scrutiny over time, the bimodal theory would support the thesis that aspects of religious experience and magical beliefs can be conceived as functions of how the mind organizes the data available to it.

10

The Unconscious and the
Science of Religion

A Summary from a Slightly Different Point of View

In 1902, James analyzed various personal accounts of religious
experience and concluded that they represented a variation
of one basic process rather than a variety of fundamentally
different experiences. Having laid this groundwork, he then
called for the establishment of a "science of religions" and
suggested that the starting point of such an endeavor might
be the consideration that the varieties of religious experience
represented "invasions from the subconscious region." He
maintained that in using this terminology we would "preserve
a contact with 'science' which the ordinary theologian lacks"
(James 1903, p. 512).

As the twentieth century began, the idea that the unconscious could be the object of scientific inquiry was viewed
as both new and exciting. Freud was then trying to create

a science that would both include an account of the unconscious and be useful in the treatment of psychiatric patients. And Myers spoke of the "subliminal self" as he carefully studied "psychic phenomena," such as trance phenomena and extrasensory perception. It was a time of intellectual ferment and exciting activity in the pursuit of the objective study of unconscious phenomena, but the anticipated fruits of this excitement only partially materialized. Myers's studies have been virtually buried in the archives, and even the psychoanalytic movement has been stymied in recent years as the public (and the insurance companies) have looked to other, less extensive forms of treatment. Since James initially called for the establishment of a "science of religions" based on a psychological look at the unconscious, there has been little popular interest in following his lead.

Almost a century has pasted since James's original remarks, and the idea of the unconscious today creates less intellectual excitement and promises fewer conceptual possibilities for future development. But I have tried, during the course of this discussion to revive its viability as a starting point for the formation of an expanded psychology where feelings would be more than merely epiphenomena of chemical and physiological processes. I have suggested a new formulation for understanding the unconscious (in terms of the two basic modes we use to process information), especially as it is contrasted with conscious awareness.

In Part One, I examined the split-brain research and the concept of symbolism. The former corroborates in experimental fashion what many thinkers from a variety of fields have suggested, viz., that there exists in the human mind two basic modes of processing information, the gestalt and the linear, collectively referred to as bimodal mental processing. To better understand these two modes, I related them to the concept of symbolism, first suggesting that the more fundamental aspect of the symbolic process is the creation of an image that functions as the symbol itself, and I suggested that this is done via the gestalt mode of processing where sensory elements are brought together instantaneously into a single form or image. But the gestalt mode of processing is involved in more than just the creation of a sensory image, for it is also involved in the synthesis of an *experiential* gestalt that includes all of our experiencing—perceptions, desires, emotions, values, and the like. There is both an integration of sensory cues into a sensory image and an integration of feelings and the entirety of experience into an experiential gestalt. There is at the same time a bringing together of these two integrations so that the sensory image symbolizes the experience. The meaning of the symbol in this case is the matrix of feelings and experiential connotations in which the symbol is embedded. In a sense, we "know" the experience of our feelings through the sensory image.

A second aspect of the symbolic process is concerned with the appreciation of relationships, especially linear ones, *between* symbols, and here the linear mode of processing is primarily involved. Through this mode we derive a rational meaning from our symbols, which depends on a certain syntax or order of presentation. The linear mode of processing is thus basic to our use of mathematics and language.

Having laid down the basic groundwork for my thesis, I then focused specifically on the significance that bimodal mental processing has for our understanding of magical thinking. Rather than look at the magical thinking of children or that of psychiatric patients, I specifically examined the language and thinking of primitive peoples because they promise the intriguing possibility of better understanding "beliefs" in the normal population, even such beliefs as those of voodoo. On this subject, I found that their language has a gestalt rather than a linear quality, the latter being characteristic of Western Indo-European languages. I speculated that the thinking and believing of these primitives reflect this quality in their language, such that they have less well-defined concepts of time, cause, and identity, concepts that we use to structure our world view and our sense of reality. For the primitive there is less separateness and distinctness of items in the world, and feelings rather than natural events seem to cause events to happen. In short, I suggest that primitive beliefs in supernatural powers, voodoo, and magic are consistent with the relative predominance of the gestalt features in their language.

Part Two progressed from magic and superstition to religion per se. I examined the implications that these ideas have for certain aspects of religion as we know it today. First I followed the lead of the philosopher Cassirer, whose scholarship suggests that in the evolution of every great religion there is a crisis where the religious leaders are able to tell the difference between a symbol and that for which the symbol stands, or, as stated in the terms of bimodal mental processing, where they are able to overcome the limitations imposed by the gestalt mode of processing. Such was the case, for instance, when Isaiah denounced as folly man's worshiping of his own creations. In this crisis adifferentiation is overcome as a people's thinking emerges from the more primitive background of magic and superstition. Second, I found that what religious scholars have called the *sine qua non* of religion, the experience of "the sacred," is characterized by the primacy of the gestalt mode in one's thinking.

This appears as a paradox, that the defining characteristic of religion is related to the primacy of the gestalt mode, yet religion per se emerges from the shadow of magic and superstition when the effects of the gestalt mode are overcome. This seems to be a contradiction, but it is not if we consider that perhaps a mature religion (to use Otto's term), as distinct from superstition and magic, depends upon a balance between the influence of the two modes of processing.

Furthermore, I have considered what James had to say about "invasions" from the unconscious, with the idea that by understanding personal religious experience in terms of the unconscious we would be using terms that are acceptable to the scientific community. James's thought has been viewed in conjunction with developments from other fields, with the hope that their combination would produce "a whole that is greater than the sum of its parts." Specifically, I have brought together James's ideas, Otto's description of "the sacred," the split-brain research, and the concept of symbolism into one understanding—a matrix that includes a psychology of the unconscious, certain aspects of religious phenomena, and research done with neurosurgical patients.

THE UNCONSCIOUS AND RELIGIOUS EXPERIENCE

Otto essentially corroborates James's thesis that there is but one basic process underlying the varieties of religious experience when he describes the experience of "the sacred" as being the essential quality of religion. Otto and James differ in that Otto considers "the sacred," as experienced in the more "evolved religions," to reflect the "actual existence" of an outside influence, while James suggests that religious experience might be "only psychological," representing "invasions" from the unconscious. (Technically, there need not necessarily be a contradiction between these two points of view, for that which is "only psychological" might also be how God makes His presence known.) However, they both testify to the idea that *one* basic process is common to all varieties of personal religious experience.

Whereas Otto describes "the wholly other" as something outside of the self, James (1903) maintains that the theologian is supported in his conviction that the religious person is moved by an external power, for it is one of the characteristics of "invasions" from the unconscious to appear objective and to arouse the feeling of an external control. James goes on to point out that in the religious perspective "the control is felt as 'higher'; but (in) our hypothesis it is primarily the higher faculties of our own hidden mind which are controlling" (p. 513). This turning away from explanations that involve supernatural forces or entities and toward an objective observation of the individual characterizes one difference between the approach of psychology as a science and the traditional approach of religion.

Otto's description of "the wholly other" and James's remarks that "invasions" from the unconscious assume the appearance of an external control find a certain concordance with a source that at first seems somewhat surprising, i.e., the split-brain experiments conducted in the last several decades by those working with neurosurgical patients being treated for intractable epilepsy. Some of these subjects, for instance, had psychological experiences which were clearly outside of their sense of self. That is, they were clearly aware of certain events, yet this awareness was just as clearly excluded from their *conscious* awareness. It is a most unusual development that one could be aware of something and yet have that something not be within one's *conscious* awareness.

"Invasions" from the unconscious, "the sacred," and now the experiences of the split-brain subjects (at least as reported verbally) all have been described as occurring outside of one's sense of self, a most curious development that suggests a relationship. A myriad of split-brain experiments have suggested that the severing of the corpus callosum demonstrates both the *functional* distinction between the two modes of mental processing as well as the *functional* distinction of the two types of awareness, a conscious awareness and an "unconscious" awareness. The suggestion is that the two modes of mental processing are in *some* way related to the two types of awareness. What we need, therefore, is a rationale for understanding how the two modes of processing might possibly be related to conscious awareness and the unconscious. That is what I attempted to do in chapter 7.

In discussing the drive to find God, the basic idea of symbolism was extended and returned us more directly to the attempt to understand "the sacred," the "wholly other," and "invasions" from the unconscious in terms consistent with the split-brain experiments. I suggested that what we call conscious awareness arises from the integration of (a) an unsymbolized awareness of sensations, feelings, and images with (b) a symbolized awareness of meanings understood in the natural language system. Furthermore, the structure characteristic of conscious awareness seems to come from two sources: the sensory perception of relationships between objects of the world, and a conceptualized understanding formulated in one's natural language system. The former, being essentially nonsymbolic, is presumably shared by our animal cousins, while the latter is a symbolic awareness that is unique to humans.

In trying to understand what occurs when one has a "religious experience," I focused on the fact that a sensory image can function in one of two ways. First, an image (or in this case, a word symbolizing the image) can function as an element in a language system, in which case it derives its meaning from the structure of the language. That is, it rests in a matrix that is more or less structured depending on whether the language itself has a more linear or more gestalt quality to it. When the linear mode predominantly influences one's language and thus one's thinking, as it generally does in Western cultures, the world and forces in the world are conceived in a relatively stable way, since time, cause, and identity are more structured. However, if the language has a more gestalt quality to it, as is the case in some primitive cultures, one conceives the world in a less structured fashion, and feelings, for instance, enter into one's sense of reality to a much greater degree.

Second, an image can symbolize a matrix of feelings connoted by the image itself. For example, as a cross might symbolize an ineffable experience for a Christian. Images acting in this way provide one of the primary avenues through which we "know" and/or express our feelings, i.e., that part of our self that has no access to sensory organs.

The key to understanding what happens when one has a "religious experience" lies in the fact that a symbol can function in either of these two ways. It can be an element within (and therefore derive its meaning from) a language system or it can derive its meaning from the matrix of feelings it connotes. On those occasions when one has a "religious experience," there is a shift in awareness from a meaning structured by linguistically organized understanding (and sensory perceptions), where the effect of feelings is minimal, to an awareness of a symbolic image and/or feelings that the image symbolizes. In this case, the awareness is for the most part unstructured. Relationships, so far as they exist at all, are defined by feelings (emotions, values, desires, etc.), and the symbolic expression of the latter are objectified, felt, and experienced as living entities, "wholly other," and outside of the self.

Much of what I have done in this investigation is to try to integrate the concept of symbolism with that of bimodal mental processing, and to consider the implications that such a combination might have for an understanding of subjective experience, especially religious experience. As I looked further, a new development emerged, one that is significant for both psychiatry and religion. Arising from the integration, the whole is found to be greater than the sum of the parts, with the whole in this case being a motivational state. This motivational state includes, among other things, the concepts of personal responsibility, behavioral commitment, and choice— concepts that indeed fall within the purview of both religion and psychology (and psychotherapy). It underlines the importance of such existential issues as values and the "meaning" to one's life, and it supplies a rationale for understanding that restless and relentless urge for human beings to satisfy their religious need—their "drive to find God."

SUBJECTIVE EXPERIENCE AND SCIENCE

If psychology is to include subjective experience per se within its domain, it must develop an approach that is consistent with the scientific demand that its theoretical constructs be tested against objective fact. Science's most successful attempt to study subjective experience has been the work of neuro-physiology. But such traditional approaches do not suffice for some experiences, as with certain psychotherapeutic or religious phenomena when one range of subjective experiences influences another. It would appear that science must either forfeit interest in such phenomena or devise an approach that is consistent with its traditional methods.

I maintain that we satisfy this demand when we examine the implications of how the human mind organizes experi-ence. That is, the science of psychology has the prerogative to examine, through traditional experimental research, how the human mind organizes experience and then to see how these fundamental processes might apply to an understanding of religious phenomena. In doing so it examines subjective experience yet grounds its logic in the hard facts of physical research. In my efforts to pursue this approach, I focused on functional (psychological) rather than anatomical distinctions, since there is still so much controversy yet to be resolved about anatomy. While the left/right anatomical distinctions of the brain are certainly oversimplifications, there is every reason to believe that the linear/gestalt functional distinction holds true, and it is the latter in which we are primarily interested here. An analysis of the split-brain research is needed on several levels: anatomical, physiological, bio-chemical, and psychological. While the issues are highly clouded on the other levels, the psychological analysis seems to hold that the human mind organizes experience via the linear and the gestalt modes of mental processing, and psy-chology need not wait until the other disciplines settle their own conflicts before exploring its own theoretical possibilities.

In the course of the discussion about religion, we were led to the subject of the unconscious, a concept that has traditionally been associated with yet another subjective area, psychotherapy. If the theory presented here is applicable to magical beliefs and religious experience, it should be equally applicable to psychotherapy. Or, to say it another way, if the human mind uses these two modes to organize religious experience, then we should see evidence that it does the same for the phenomena of psychotherapy. And this is indeed what we found in a variety of instances. Moreover, because bimodal mental processing is part of a larger picture that includes predictability and usefulness within psychiatry, its viability as a basis for understanding magical beliefs and religious experience is enhanced. Perhaps eventually we may see a "science of religions" based on the concept of the unconscious, something James envisioned so many years ago.

HUMAN PASSION AND HUMAN SCIENCE

There is something about the word *humanism* that is anathema to many churchmen. Undoubtedly there is the apprehension that human decency and Judeo-Christian values will disappear from social intercourse if the human being is the center of human interest. But when the clergy insist on removing the human being from the center of interest, they miss the opportunity to find evidence from "natural" sources that would support and reinforce religious values as well as a classical religious orientation to life. But is there any reason to believe that religious intuition is so out of phase with life that it would find *no* concordance with nature itself, within the human mind? I think not. Perhaps religious values reside within us and rise from the unconscious to become objectified in our conscious awareness. Cassirer suggested this long ago when he put forth the idea that religious phenomena were forms of the mind's symbolic expression. I suspect that a "natural" look at the human being will support and reinforce certain classical religious values, such as love and concern for one's fellow beings. (Certainly Maslow thought that to be the case and he felt he demonstrated it in his research.)

This discussion has looked at the human being with the idea that eventually there may in fact be a concordance between human passions, including religious passions, and human science. Religious values may be both understood and justified by science. Such cannot be the case, however, unless science expands into areas traditionally left to religion, unless science becomes complete by including the nonrational and ex- periential within its domain. Its formulations will be dry and sterile compared to the passions of religious expression, but such formulations will perhaps allow for the possibility of expressing the human logical faculty as it becomes consonant with religious passions, something that is needed if we are to have a unity of thought.

In his anthology *The Perennial Philosophy,* Huxley pointed out that in every major religion of the world, as well as in the traditional lore of primitive people in every region of the world, there is a recurrent pattern of belief—the psychology that one finds in the individual "something simi- lar to, or even identical with, divine Reality" (p. vii). The mere fact that such a pattern within nature (within the subjective beliefs of human beings) is so recurrent is enough to arouse the curiosity of the scientist. But to study this recurring form (belief) one must develop a credible approach to such matters. This is what I have attempted to do here. From a natural point of view, the observation made by Huxley would suggest that we could find within human beings something paralleling nature, an intriguing idea in itself. From the point of view of science, the question arises as to whether there is perhaps a concordance between the two modes of processing information and the information from the world to be processed. Does the world present itself in two different modes? From the perspective of religion it should be equally exciting, perhaps enough to motivate an objective look at the human need (drive) to "find God." Certainly the mystics of every age looked within (as did the psychologists Jung and James). If ever passion and reason are to be made consonant, the effort must start by looking rationally at the nonrational aspects of humankind. If ever there is developed a theology credible to an empiricist, I would think it must start with ideas and concepts similar to those presented here.

Appendices

I

Certainty, Uncertainty, and Complementarity as They Relate to Bimodal Mental Processing

After I had finished the body of this book, I was privileged to an exchange of letters and ideas with Dr. George Engel, professor emeritus in the departments of medicine and psychiatry at the University of Rochester School of Medicine. We discussed a number of issues related to both his work and my own, among which was the question of certainty and uncertainty in science generally and psychiatry in particular. In this correspondence, we discussed Heisenberg's uncertainty principle as well as Bohr's ideas about complementarity. During the course of our exchange, Dr. Engel urged me to include an appendix that would discuss how bimodal processing relates to these two issues. Thus, in response to his encouragement and support, I offer the following.

Heisenberg (1927) discovered that the precision of measurement in empirical science has a limit, and that even in principle one cannot precisely measure subatomic particles beyond the order of Planck's constant, h. Since the time of its original formulation, the uncertainty principle has received much attention. One corollary to Heisenberg's ideas was proposed by Bohr who suggested that the uncertainty principle is only a special case of a broader principle that pervades all human knowledge (Folse, 1985). He called this broader framework "complementarity," since it was based on the idea that there are times when human understanding—in terms of the classical concepts of time, space—and causality proves inadequate. When this occurs the mind requires two antithetical points of view if understanding is to take place, points of view that are complementary and cannot be reduced to the other. This is the case, for example, when the process of observation affects what is being observed. The wave and the particle theories of light, for instance, would serve as a special example of this broader viewpoint.

I became aware of Bohr's ideas rather late in the game, but when I realized that his view suggested that complementarity was an outgrowth of the basic limitations of the human mind, I was intrigued. I naturally wondered just how his ideas relate to the two modes of mental processing, since I have suggested they impose limits on (or perhaps reflect limits that are inherent in) how the human mind organizes data.

In an effort to elaborate on these last remarks, I will make a small detour to assure that I am understood. First, I start from Kant's (1896) premise that the human mind is not passive but actively participates in the organization of data, taking the myriad of accessible sensory cues and organizing them into a meaningful whole. Second, there is ample evidence that the human mind cannot find meaning in just any form, but finds symbolic expression and meaning in two distinctly different ways, the gestalt and the linear modes of mental processing. Some experiences are better expressed in the former mode, while other experiences are better expressed in the latter. For instance, the feelings evoked by Van Gogh's last painting of crows over a cornfield, completed just before his suicide, are expressed in a vibrant and disturbing way—far better than any discursive discussion could ever do. And no painting could ever approach the precision of an algebraic equation. Each experience has its own form of expression.

Kant maintained that the senses of time, space, and cause are a priori, while the concepts of unity, necessity, reciprocal relationships, and so on, are among the basic categories of reason through which the mind organizes experience. However, Kant was at this point considering only certain aspects of human experience, those that lend themselves to expression in the linear form. It remained for the philosopher Cassirer to draw attention to those aspects of human experience that are best expressed symbolically in the gestalt mode, experiences that do not lend themselves to linear expression.

As Kant suggested, the human mind never knows the "thing-in-itself": it only knows its own experience of the world, and this, as I have suggested, is limited to only certain forms. The self, for instance, might be experienced subjectively as feelings, or it might be conceived in thoughts and concepts. Both ways of "knowing" the self are legitimate, but neither can be reduced to the other. Both reflect a more basic phenomenon, and it takes both experiences to identify adequately that which we call the self.

CERTAINTY AND UNCERTAINTY

In light of the above, let us examine what the two modes of mental processing might have to do with certainty and uncertainty. First, one aspect having to do exclusively with the linear mode needs to be mentioned. It is the old addage that insofar as we are certain of the truth of a theory it does not apply to reality, and insofar as a theory applies to reality we are not certain of its truth. This, of course, relates to the limitations of deductive and inductive reason, which add uncertainty to what human beings can rationally accomplish. This point is pertinent to a discussion of certainty and uncertainty and is deserving of mention, but it is not the point to be discussed here.

The concept of certainty (as opposed to a feeling), like the concepts of cause and time and Kant's other categories, has meaning that is restricted to the linear mode. (Of course, one might say that all concepts have meaning restricted to the linear form since all concepts are best expressed in the linear form of language, but that is not what I mean here.) The concept of certainty implies that something is certain in relation to something else, and I maintain that the ability to isolate and separate an item and to compare it with something else is characteristic of the linear mode of processing, and inherently absent in the gestalt mode.

The same can be said of uncertainty, since this term describes that which is not beyond doubt. And this, as simple as it may sound, has interesting consequences. For instance, those aspects of human experience in which meaning can best be expressed using the gestalt form—such as the feelings expressed by Van Gogh's painting—if viewed from the linear perspective might be said to be "uncertain" because of the absence of certainty, i.e., the absence of the means to isolate and compare and thus the absence of certainty. Actually, in this situation certainty and uncertainty are not so much absent as lacking in meaning, and while the absence of the former might by default suggest the presence of the latter, in truth neither concept has meaning. They just do not pertain. In short, both certainty and uncertainty seem to be concepts, like time and cause, that the mind uses when it looks at itself and the world from the scientific, logical, postivistic, "Western," linear perspective. But this leaves out a vast ocean of experience that can best be expressed via the gestalt mode where certainty and uncertainty have no meaning.

Now I assume that in the human mind the two modes of mental processing always work together and that there is virtually no occasion where the two do not operate simultaneously. (And when I say "working together" I do not mean in a homogenized way where the two modes are lost within a blend; I mean in a way whereby each process uses what the other has to offer for its own ends. I think there is ample evidence for separate processes.) With this assumption, then, it follows that from the linear perspective *uncertainty is inherent in all human experience.* That is, because the gestalt mode is involved in all human experience, and because certainty is inherently absent in that mode, if one observes from the classical "Western," logical, and (more certain) linear perspective (where something is uncertain if certainty is absent), then human experience is inherently uncertain, whether it be that of the physicist with his particle accelerators or the psychiatrist with his psychodynamic formulations.

From this perspective the uncertainty principle, as articulated by Heisenberg, may be a special case of a more generic uncertainty, resulting from the limitations imposed by the way in which the mind organizes experience. It should be pointed out, however, that this uncertainty has meaning only within the linear point of view. All of this may sound quite complicated, but the gist of the matter is that a part of us (the part that views things from a linear perspective) craves what it cannot have, i.e., certainty. It cannot be had because neither nature nor human experience is so simple.

This brings us to yet another point, the relationship between the feelings of certainty and uncertainty and their respective concepts; and this in turn takes us into the realm of beliefs, an area that has defied all attempts at definition. With this caveat, let us go on. From what has been said it follows that believing (having a belief) entails the complementary action of the two modes of mental processing. Gestalt integrations are processed in a linear fashion and linearly processed symbols are integrated in a gestalt fashion, etc., etc., etc. Our feelings, symbolized as gestalt images, are in this way incorporated into our beliefs, and this process eventually involves our natural language system. Without these feelings, our beliefs would be lifeless and would have no emotional depth. Without the structure of our natural language system there would be no stability or firmness or continuity. This world view, this matrix of feelings and structure, is the basis for our beliefs and gives rise to a feeling of certainty or uncertainty, depending upon its own internal consistency and the intensity of the emotions evoked at any one time.

COMPLEMENTARITY

In light of all this, it seems natural to suggest that the two modes of mental processing are complementary to one another in the way that Bohr intended. Or one could say that being aware of perceptions and feelings on an unsymbolized level is complementary to being aware of symbolic meanings. Ideally, feelings and rational thinking should work together and coincide; and from what has previously been said, it appears that when they do not there is cognitive dissonance.

The core of Bohr's ideas about complementarity, when applied to psychology, rests on the difference between conscious awareness subjectively experienced and conscious awareness as an object of description. As Bohr pointed out, as soon as one tries to define conscious awareness objectively it ceases to be experienced subjectively, and it was his point that in such a case the process of observation affects what is being observed. This of course is analagous to the situation in physics where the process of measuring subatomic particles affects the measurement of them. And it was from this insight that he suggested that for something so affected, whether in physics or psychology, one needs two complementary views or descriptions. In physics it would mean conceiving of an electron both as a particle and as a wave. Both theories seem necessary to describe the underlying reality that neither can adequately reflect individually, yet the two theories contradict one another. Neither is a complete description of reality, and this dual theory seems the best the human mind can do in grappling with what it cannot directly grasp.

So too is the case for the human psyche. Human behavior, for instance, might be understood in terms of the subjective feeling of freedom to act, or in terms of the act itself being part of an endless chain of causal events. And just like the particle and wave theories in physics, neither the feeling of freedom nor the chain of causal events adequately reflects reality. It takes the two together to describe the unseen reality that gives rise to both impressions. And like the wave and the particle theories in physics, these two ideas seem to conflict—one describing freedom and the other denying it—yet neither alone is adequate in its description of reality.

From Bohr's viewpoint we see here an obvious "bifurcation" of the human psyche. The idea that the mind orders part of itself via a chain of causal events is an obvious reference to the linear mode. And feelings, Bohr's other great division of mind, are best expressed symbolically via the gestalt mode. The two modes of mental processing are therefore complementary in their symbolic expression of human experience. We already knew that, of course, but now we also know that they are complementary even in Bohr's sense of the term.

II

Feeling and Structure

Descartes, on a cold November night in 1619, discovered the fundamental accord between reason and the laws of nature, and that experience emphasized the Western world's appreciation of the structural or organizational component of the mind's world view. For centuries thereafter, the Western mind continued to be enamored of this aspect of its experience and almost excluded everything else from legitimacy. In doing so it ignored the feeling component of one's experience of the world, the color and life of emotions, values, desires, and the like. This latter component reflects the emotional and feeling experience of the individual himself and it underscores the point that one's world view represents both the world and the individual. It represents one's own personal interpretation of the world, one's own values and significance, as well as the objects and structure of the world itself.

Stated most simply, one's world view has two components: feeling and structure. The feeling component is symbolized by feeling laden images, and the structure is a function of

235

the relatively constant relationships of the sensory images of the world itself and those symbolic meanings that the mind organizes via its language faculty. The mind organizes images through the process of "thinking," and the use of words allows this thinking to assume the form of language, where in Western Indo-European languages words are related in a certain syntax or linear order and thus convey a meaning. (It should be pointed out that one can relate images in two ways. They can be related through feelings: i.e., if the connotations of feelings are similar or the same for two images, they can be equated or condensed into one form. They can also be related through syntax as we primarily do in Western Indo-European languages. This is the difference between the psychoanalysts' primary process and secondary process thinking.) These meanings can in turn be symbolized by other words that in turn can be related so as to create new meanings, and so on. Through such an epigenetic construction a matrix of understanding is formed, one that is based on a natural language system. I maintain that what we experience as conscious awareness is a product of the integration of (a) our unsymbolized experience of sensations, feelings, and sensory perceptions, with (b) our symbolized understanding as structured by our natural language system. Exactly how these components are mediated, whether as a whole or through separate parallel systems, will have to be decided by others.

One might be tempted to equate the feeling and the structure of our world view with the gestalt and the linear modes of mental processing, but this would not be accurate. Instead, to reiterate, it would seem that the structure of one's world view arises from the integration of (a) the spatially structured but unsymbolized experience of perceptual forms with (b) a structured understanding based on our natural language system.

III

"Knowing" and Sensory Images

Common sense suggests that an individual "knows" the world by incorporating sensory images within the self. That is, he or she "knows" a tree when it is seen. But this is more than common sense it seems, for on looking at the roots of our philosophical heritage, we find a curious thing. Quoting Chessick (1986), who was referring to Heidegger's work:

> The Greek verb, εἴδω, means "I see." The future εἴσομαι, I will see; the past εἴδον, I saw. Then curiously in the second perfect, ὀίδα, which should be "I have seen," it changes meaning in Greek to "I know." It becomes a present tense of the verb "I know." The pluperfect, ἤδη, which should be "I had seen," becomes "I knew." (p. 90)

All this suggests, of course, that what we experience as "knowing" is somehow related to sensory images. This is rather clear with such words as *tree* or *chair* or even with such metaphorical expressions as the "head" of a pin or "bringing" something "to a head," but what about words and expressions that seem to have no obvious sensory referent? Could it be that such words and expressions were once based on sensory experiences that have, over time, receded into the background and dropped from awareness? There are those who think so. Arendt (1977) observes:

> No language has a ready-made vocabulary for the needs of mental activity; they all borrow their vocabulary from words originally meant to correspond either to sense experience or to other experiences of ordinary life. (p. 102)

Jaynes (1976, p. 69) pointed out that "psyche," the word that later came to mean soul or conscious mind, originally meant life-substances, such as the blood that the dying warrior bleeds out onto the ground or the breath he breaths out with his last gasp. Jaynes pointed out that the verb "to be" originally came from the Sanskrit word meaning "to grow" and "is" evolved from the same root as the Sanskrit word "to breath."

> It comes as a lovely surprise that the irregular conjugation of our most nondescript verb is thus a record of a time when man had no independent word for "existence" and could only say that something "grows" or that is "breathes." (Jaynes 1976, p. 51)

References

Alajouanine, T. 1948. Aphasia and artistic realization. *Brain 71*:229–241.

Alema, G.; Rosadine, G.; and Rossi, G. 1961. Psychic reactions associated with intracarotid amytal injection and relation to brain damage. *Excerpta Medica 37*:154–155.

Arendt, H. 1971. *The Life of the mind.* San Diego, New York, and London: Harcourt Brace Jovanovich.

Bandler, R., and Grinder, J. 1975. *The Structure of magic.* Palo Alto: Science and Behavior Books,

Bateson, G., and Jackson, D. 1964, Some varieties of pathogenic organization. *Research Publications—Association for Research in Nervous and Mental Disease 42*:270–283.

Beaumont, J. G., and Dimond S. J. 1973. Brain disconnection and schizophrenia. *British Journal of Psychiatry 123*:661–662.

Becker, E. 1973. *The Denial of death.* New York: The Free Press, Macmillan Publishing Co., Inc.

Benson, D. F., and Zaidel, E., eds. 1985. *The Dual brain.* New York and London: The Guilford Press,

Benton, A. L., and Joynt, R. J. 1960. Early descriptions of aphasia. *Archives of Neurology 3*:205–222.

Blass, E. M. 1976. *The Psychobiology of Curt Richter.* Baltimore: York Press.

Bogan, J. E., 1973. The Other side of the brain: An Appositional mind. In Ornstein, 1973.

Bogan, J. E., and Gazzangia, M. S. 1965. Cerebral commissurotomy in man: Minor hemisphere dominance for certain visuospatial functions. *Journal of Neurosurgery 23:*394-399.

Brehm, J. W., and Cohen, A. R. 1962. *Exploration in cognitive dissonance.* New York: Wiley.

Cannon, W. B. 1942. Voodoo death. *American Anthropologist 44:*169.

Cassirer, E. 1955. *The Philosophy of symbolic forms, Volume 2 mythical thought.* New Haven and London: Yale University Press.

Chase, R. A. 1966. The Effect of temporal lobe lesions on some auditory information processing tasks in man. In Darley, 1966.

Chessick, R. D. 1986. Heidegger for psychotherapists. *American Journal of Psychotherapy 40:*83-95.

Chomsky, N. 1957. *The Syntactic structures.* The Hague: Mouton.

Critchley, M. 1966. *The Parietal lobes.* London: E. Arnold. (Originally printed in 1953.)

Darley, F. L., ed. 1966. *Brain mechanisms underlying speech and language.* New York: Grune and Stratton.

d'Elia, G., and Perris, C. 1973. Cerebral functional dominance and depression. *Acta Psychiatrica Scandinavica 49:*191-197.

———. 1974. Cerebral functional dominance and memory functions: An analysis of EEG integrated amplitude in depressive psychotics. *Acta Psychiatrica Scandinavica, Supplement* 143-157.

Descartes, R. 1958. *Philosophical writings.* Translated by N. K. Smith. New York: Random House, The Modern Library.

Deutsch, D., ed. 1982. *The Psychology of music.* New York: Academic Press.

Dimond, S., and Farrington, L. 1977. Cited in Restak 1984, p. 263.

Eddington, A. S. 1929. *The Nature of the physical world.* New York: Macmillan; Cambridge: The University Press.

Eliade, M. 1959. *The Sacred and the profane.* New York: Harcourt Brace Jovanovich.

Ettlinger, E. G.; Reuck, V. S.; and Porter. R., eds. 1965. *Functions of the corpus callosum.* Boston: Little, Brown.

Fenichel, O. 1945. *The Psychoanalytic theory of neurosis.* New York: Norton.

Ferenczi, S. 1926. *Further contributions to the theory and technique of psyohoanalysis.* London: Hogarth Press.

Festinger, L. 1957. *A Theory of cognitive dissonance.* Stanford, Calif.: Stanford University Press.

Folse, H. J. 1985. *The Philosophy of Neils Bohr: The framework of complementarity.* Amsterdam: North Holland.

Foucault, M. 1973. *The Birth of the clinic.* New York: Pantheon Books.

Freud, S. 1946. *Collected papers, Volume IV.* London: Hogarth Press.

———. 1954. Project for a scientific psychology. In *Origins of psychoanalysis: Letters to Wilhelm Fliess, drafts and notes, 1887–1902.* New York: Basic Books.

———. 1961. *Standard edition of the complete psychological works.* London: Hogarth.

Gainotti, G. 1967. Reactions "catastrophiques" et manifestations d'indifference au cours des atteintes cerebrales. *Neuropsychologia 7:*195–204.

Galin, D. 1974. Implications for psychiatry of left and right cerebral specialization. *Archives of General Psychiatry 31:*572–583.

———. 1988. Conceptual and methodological issues in neuropsychological studies of depression. In M. Kinsbourne, ed., 1988.

Gardner, H. 1983. *Frames of mind.* New York: Basic Books.

Gazzaniga, M. S. 1973. The Split brain in man. In Ornstein, 1973.

———. 1985. *The Social brain: Discovering the networks of mind.* New York: Basic Books.

Gazzaniga, M. S.; Bogan, J. E.; and Sperry, R. W. 1965. Observations on visual perception after disconnection of the cerebral hemispheres in man. *Brain 88 (2):*221–236.

Gazzaniga, M. S., and LeDoux, J. E. 1978. *The Integrated mind.* New York: Plenum Press.

Gazzaniga, M. S., and Young, E. D. 1967. Effects of commissurotomy on the processing of increasing visual information. *Experimental Brain Research 3:*368–371.

Glic, S. S.; Jerussi, T. P.; and Zimmerberg, B. 1977. Behavioral and neuropharmacological correlates of nigrostriatal asymmetry in rats. In S. Harnad, R. W. Doty, L. Goldstein, J. Jaynes, and G. Krauthamer, 1977.

Globus, G. G.; Maxwell, G.; and Savodnik, I., eds. 1976. *Consciousness and the brain.* New York and London: Plenum Press.

Goldstein, K. 1960. Thinking and speaking. *Annals of the New York Academy of Science 91:*38–51.

Green, P. 1978. Defective interhemispheric transfer in schizophrenia. *Journal of Abnormal Psychology 87:*472–480.

Gruzelier, J. 1981. Cerebral laterality and psychopathology: Fact and fiction. *Psychological Medicine 11:*219–227.

Gruzelier, J., and Venables, P. 1974. Bimodality and lateral asymmetry of skin conductance orienting activity in schizophrenics: Replication and evidence of lateral asymmetry in patients with depression and disorders of personality. *Biological Psychiatry 8:*55–73.

Gur, R. E. 1978. Left hemisphere dysfunction and left hemisphere overactivation in schizophrenia. *Journal of Abnormal Psychology 87:*226–238.

———. 1977. Motoric laterality imbalance in schizophrenia. *Archives of General Psychiatry 34:*33–37.

Harnad, S.; Doty, R. W.; Goldstein, L.; Jaynes, J.; and Krauthamer, G., eds. 1977. *Lateralization in the nervous system.* New York: Academic Press.

Head, H. 1963. *Aphasia and kindered disorders of speech, Volume 1.* New York: Hafner, reprint of 1926 edition.

Hebb, D. O. 1955. Drives and the C.N.S. *Psychological Review 62:*243–254.

Hecaen, H., and de Ajuriaguerra, J. 1964. *Lefthandedness.* New York: Grune & Stratten.

Hecaen, H., de Ajuriaguerra, J., and Angelergues, R. 1963. Apraxia and its various aspects. In L. Halpern, 1963.

Heilbroner, R. 1980. *An Inquiry into the human prospect: Updated and reconsidered for the 1980's.* New York: Norton.

Heisenberg, W. 1927. Uber den Anschaulichen inhalt den quantentheoretischen kinematick and mechanik. *Leitschift fur Physik 43:*172–188.

Henschen, S. E. 1926. On the Function of the right hemisphere of the brain in relation to the left in speech, music, and calculation. *Brain 49:*110–123.

Hoffman, B. 1972. *Albert Einstein creator and rebel.* New York: New American Library.

Horowitz, M. 1972. Modes of representation of thought. *Journal of the American Psychoanalytic Association 20:*793–819.

Hume, D. 1888. *A Treatise of human nature.* Ed. by L. A. Selby-Bigge. (Originally published 1739 & 1740, Oxford: Clarendon Press.)

Humphrey, M. E., and Zangwill, O. L. 1951. Cessation of dreaming after brain injury. *Journal of Neurology, Neurosurgery, and Psychiatry 14:*322–325.

Huxley, A. 1970. *The Perennial philosophy*. New York: Harper and Row.

James, W. 1890. *The Principles of psychology*. New York: Henry Holt.
———. 1903. *The Varieties of religious experience: A study of human nature*. New York: Longman, Green, and Co.
———. 1974. The Will to believe. Published in *Essays on faith and morals*. New York: New American Library.
Jaynes, J. 1976. *The Origins of consciousness in the breakdown of the bicameral mind*. Boston: Houghton Mifflin.
Jones, E. 1929. Fear, guilt and hate. *International Journal of Psychoanalysis 10*:383–397.
Jung, C. G. 1963. *Memories, dreams, and reflections*. New York: Pantheon Books. Random House.

Kant, I. 1896. *Critique of pure reason*. Translated by F. Max Müller (originally published in 1794). New York: Macmillan.
Keller, H. 1936. *The Story of my life*. Garden City: Doubleday, Doran & Co. (first edition 1902).
Kernberg, O. 1980. *Internal world and external reality*. New York and London: Jason Aronson.
Kimura, D. 1964. Left–Right differences in the perception of melodies. *Quarterly Journal of Experimental Psychology 16*: 355–358.
Kinsbourne, M. ed. 1988. *Cerebral hemisphere function in depression*. Washington: American Psychiatric Press.
Kohler, W. 1925. *The Mentality of apes*. London: K. Paul, Trench, Trubner & Co.; New York: Harcourt, Brace & Co.
Kuhn, T. 1970. *The Structure of scientific revolutions*. 2nd Ed., Chicago: University of Chicago Press.

Langer, S. 1980. *Philosophy in a new key*. Cambridge, Mass.: Harvard University Press (first edition, 1942).

Lee, D. 1973. Codification of reality: Lineal and nonlineal. In Ornstein, 1973, pp. 128–142.

Levinson, P. ed. 1982. *In the Pursuit of truth: Essays on the philosophy of Karl Popper on the occasion of his eightieth birthday.* Sussex: Harvester Press.

Levi-Strauss, C. 1966. *The Savage mind.* Chicago: University of Chicago Press.

Levy-Bruhl, L. 1928. *The "Soul" of the primitive.* London: George Allen and Unwin.

————. 1975. *The Notebooks on primitive mentality.* New York, Evanston, San Francisco: Harper and Row Publishing.

————. 1978. *Primitive mentality.* New York: AMS Press.

Luria, A. R. 1966. *Higher cortical functions in man.* New York: Basic Books.

————. 1966. *Human brain and psychological processes.* New York: Harper Row.

Luria, A. R.; Tsvetkova, L. S.; and Futer, D. S. 1965. Aphasia in a composer. *Journal of the Neurological Sciences 2*:288–292.

Mandell, A. 1985. Interhemispheric fusion. *Journal of Psychoactive Drugs 17*(4):257–266.

Marin, O. S. M. 1982. Neurological aspects of music perception and performance. In D. Deutsch, 1982, pp. 453–477.

Maslow, A. H. 1964. *Religions, values and peak-experiences.* Ohio State University Press.

Maxwell, C. 1873. *A Treatise on electricity and magnetism.* Oxford: Clarendon Press.

Millikan, D., and Darley, F., eds. 1967. *Brain mechanisms underlying speech and language.* New York: Grune & Stratton.

Milner, B. 1962. Laterality effects in audition. In V. B. Mountcastle, 1962.

————. 1967. Cited in Rossi, G. and Rosadini, G., Experimental analysis of cerebral dominance in man. In D. Millikan and F. Darley, 1967.

Mountcastle, V. B., ed. 1962. *Interhemispheric relations and cerebral dominance.* Baltimore: Johns Hopkins Press.

Myers, F. W. H. 1903. *Human personality and its survival of bodily death,* Volume I, London, New York, and Bombay: Longman, Green, and Co.

———. 1903. *Human personality and its survival of bodily death,* Volume II, London, New York, and Bombay: Longman, Green, and Co.

Myers, R. E. 1965. The Neocortical commissures and interhemispheric transmission of information. In E. G. Ettlinger, A. V. Reuck, and R. Porter, eds., 1965.

Myers, R. E., and Sperry, R. W. 1953. Interocular transfer of a visual form discrimination habit in cats after section of the optic chiasma and corpus callosum. *Anatomical Record 115:* 351–352.

Myslobodsky, M. S., and Horesh, N. 1978. Bilateral electrodermal activity in depressive patients. *Biological Psychiatry 6:*111–120.

Nieoullon, A.; Cheramy, A.; and Glowinski, J. 1978. Release of dopamine in both caudate nuclei and both substantia nigra in response to unilateral stimulation of cerebellar nuclei in the cat. *Brain Research 148:*143–152.

Northrop, F. S. C. 1979. *The Meeting of east and west.* Woodbridge, Conn.: Ox Bow Press (first published in 1946).

Ornstein, R. E. 1972. *The Psychology of consciousness.* New York: Penguin Books.

———., ed. 1973. *The Nature of human consciousness.* New York: W. H. Freeman.

Otto, R. 1982. *The Idea of the holy.* London: Oxford University Press (first published in 1917).

Perls, F. 1971. *Gestalt therapy verbatim.* Toronto, New York, London: Bantam Books.

Planck, M. 1915. *Eight lectures on theoretical physics.* New York: Columbia University Press.

Poincare, H. 1952. *Science and method.* Translated by F. Maitland. New York: Dover.

Polanyi, M. 1958. *Personal knowledge: Towards a post-critical philosophy.* Chicago: University of Chicago Press.

————. 1974. Faith and reason. In Schwartz, 1974, pp. 116–130. (First published in *Journal of Religion 41:*237–247.)

Pribram, K. H. 1962. (Untitled discussion.) In V. B. Montcastle, ed., 1962.

————. 1976. Problems concerning the structure of consciousness. In G. G. Globus, G. Maxwell, and I. Savodnik, eds., 1976, pp. 297–313.

Quarton, G. C.; Melnechuck, T.; and Schmitt, F. O., eds. 1967. *The Neurosciences: A study program.* New York: Rockefeller University Press.

Ravetz, J. 1971. *Scientific knowledge and its social problems.* Oxford: Clarendon Press.

Restak, R. 1984. *The Brain.* Toronto: Bantam Books.

Richter, C. 1976. On the Phenomenon of sudden death in animals and man. In Blass 1976, pp. 319–329. [First published in *Psychosomatic Medicine 19(3)* (May–June) 1957.]

Roemer, R. A.; Shagass, C.; Straumanis, J. J.; and Amadeo, M. 1978. Pattern evoked potential measurements suggesting lateralized hemispheric dysfunction in chronic schizophrenics/ *Biological Psychiatry 12:*185–202.

Rossi, G., and Rosadini, G. 1967. Experimental analysis of cerebral dominance in man. In D. Millikan and F. Darley, 1967.

Ruesch, J., and Kees, W. 1956. *Nonverbal communication.* Berkeley: University of California Press.

Russell, B. 1974. *Religion and science.* Oxford: Oxford University Press (first published in 1935 by Home University Library).

Schwartz, F., ed. 1974. *Scientific thought and social reality: Essays by Michael Polanyi.* New York: International University Press.

Shankiweiler, D. 1966. Effects of temporal lobe damage on perception of dichotically presented melodies. *Journal of Comparative Physiological Psychology 62:*115–119.

Smith, H. 1952. *Man and his gods.* Boston: Little, Brown, and Co.

Sperry, R. W. 1961. Cerebral organization and behavior. *Science 133:*1749–1757.

———. 1964. The Great cerebral commissure. *Scientific American* (January):42–52.

———. 1967. Split-brain approach to learning problems. In G. C. Quarton, T. Melnechuck, and F. O. Schmitt, eds., 1967.

———. 1968. Hemisphere deconnection and unity in conscious awareness. *American Psychologist 23:*723–733.

———. 1976. Mental phenomena as causal determinants in brain function. In G. G. Globus, G. Maxwell, and I. Savodnik, eds., 1976, pp. 163–177.

———. 1985. Consciousness, personal identity, and the divided brain. In Benson and Zaidel, eds., 1985.

Springer, S. P., and Deutsch, G. 1981. *Left brain, right brain.* New York and San Francisco: W. H. Freeman and Co.

Trevarthen, C. B. 1962. Double visual learning in split-brain monkeys. *Science 136:*258–259.

Waters, F. 1963. *Book of the Hopi.* New York: Viking Press.

Wertheim, N., and Botez, M. I. 1961. Receptive amusia: A clinical analysis. *Brain 84:*19–30.

Wexler, B. 1980. Cerebral laterality and psychiatry: A review of the literature. *American Journal of Psychiatry 137:*279–291.

———. 1988. Regional brain dysfunction in depression. In M. Kinsbourne, ed., 1988.

Wexler, B. E., and Heninger, G. R. 1979. Alteration in cerebral laterality in acute psychotic illness. *Archives of General Psychiatry 36*:278.

Wicklund, R. A., and Brehm, J. W. 1976. *Perspectives on cognitive dissonance.* Hillsdale, New Jersey: Lawrence Erlbaum Assoc.

Name Index

251

Subject Index

255